Principles of Deliverance: You Can be Set Free from Demonic Forces

Authored by E.A. Windischman

ISBN-13: 978-0692640197
ISBN-10: 0692640193
The Kingdom Paradigm, LLC

Library of Congress Control Number: 2016902359

© 2016 By E.A. Windischman

The Kingdom Paradigm, LLC
Woodridge, IL

The Bible text designated KJV is from the 1769 *Authorized Version*, commonly known as the *King James Version*.

Scripture quotations marked NLT are taken from the *Holy Bible, New Living Translation*, copyright (c) 1996. Used by permission of Tyndale House Publishers, Inc., Wheaton, Illinois 60189. All rights reserved.

Scripture marked NKJV is taken from the *New King James Version*®. Copyright © 1982 by Thomas Nelson. Used by permission. All rights reserved.

Dedication

This book is dedicated to the memory of my dear sister Jenny. Peace and freedom can sometimes be elusive, so in identifying the two primary sources of our fallen human condition, and God's given resolution, my prayer is that all who read find the peace and liberty that can only be found in Jesus Christ.

Contents

DEDICATION	2
CONTENTS	3
PREFACE - A PERSONAL NOTE	4
PRINCIPLE ONE: GOD LOVES YOU!	14
PRINCIPAL TWO: UNDERSTAND THE BIG MESS	21
PRINCIPLE THREE: UNDERSTAND THE ENEMY	28
PRINCIPLE FOUR: UNDERSTAND SINS CONSEQUENCE	34
PRINCIPLE FIVE: UNDERSTAND THE HOLY ANGELS	37
PRINCIPLE SIX: UNDERSTAND GOD'S PROMISE	47
PRINCIPLE TWO CONTINUED: DOWNWARD TREND	52
PRINCIPLE SEVEN: UNDERSTAND GOD'S KINGDOM	66
PRINCIPLE EIGHT: UNDERSTAND WHY CHRIST CAME – PART 1	70
PRINCIPLE EIGHT: UNDERSTAND WHY CHRIST CAME – PART 2	89
PRINCIPLE NINE: OCCULT OPENS DOORS TO DEMONIC	95
PRINCIPLE ONE REVISITED: GOD LOVES US	103
PRINCIPLE NINE CONTINUED: WRONG THEN, WRONG TODAY	105
PRINCIPLE TEN: ONLY SINNERS CAN BE SET FREE BY CHRIST	125
HOW TO BE SET FREE	131
PROCLAMATION OF DELIVERANCE	139
SCRIPTURAL PASSAGES FOR MEMORY AND MEDITATION	144
CONCLUSION	152
REMEDIAL GLOSSARY OF BIBLICAL TERMS	157
ENDNOTES AND BIBLIOGRAPHY	183

Preface - A Personal Note

Before we explore what the Bible teaches about the serious subject of deliverance, I want the reader to understand that I know Christ can set you free from evil spirits, because he has set me free from evil spirits! When I was a young adult, he set me free from a demonic addiction I had to a controlled substance. The heavenly Father has also allowed me the privilege of assisting others to be set free from the forces of darkness, by sharing the good news of Jesus Christ, and by direct confrontation of evil spirits in the authority of Jesus mighty name.

Any person that truly comes to God in faith has to confront his or her own personal sins, failings, and spiritual struggles. I am no exception, nor will you be. However, in addition to allowing God's Holy Spirit to reveal to us our true condition before Him so we can accept his offer of new life in Christ, allowing Him to build in us godly character and virtue, we also need to realize that **living on the earth in this current evil age places us in the midst of intense spiritual conflict**. There is a battle for our very souls and eternity hangs in the balance!

Unmasking the Enemy

Please allow me to share an experience I had while a bible school student in the mid 1980's.

During the Passover season of 1986 I was living in Israel as a student in the Arava desert. I took the week we had off to attend a conference on prophecy being held in Jerusalem. The "Jerusalem Gathering" sponsored by what was at that time a fledgling British publication "Prophecy Today" (now an online publication) included speakers such as Cecil Kerr, Clifford Hill, and Lance Lambert.

I had been in prayer and fasting for several days in preparation for the event. During one of the sessions being held at the Binyanei HaOoma Convention Center, someone a few rows in front of me kept coughing during most of the session. The minister facilitating the session had a penetrating word of knowledge that God wanted to heal someone with a cough and pointed in the area where the source of the disturbance was coming from. Something in my spirit, being more sensitized due to my fast, knew there was more than a simple cough that needed to be addressed.

After the session, while people were leaving the auditorium, I remained in my seat to pray and fellowship with our Creator, and meditate on what had been presented in the session. I thought the theatre was empty, when all of a sudden I heard that same coughing coming from the balcony section, and someone saying with authority, "In the name of Jesus, I command you to come out!" I immediately began interceding in prayer for the situation. Then, a moment later, I heard a piercing scream that seemed to bounce off the walls of the great theatre, not so much like an echo, but rather like a trapped animal looking for a way of escape. Then there was a brief silence followed by the sound of a woman weeping, and the comforting words of the voice I had heard commanding the demon to leave a few moments earlier, and the voice of another person also offering soothing words. I got up to leave, and later had a brief conversation with the person who had ministered deliverance to the woman. The woman indeed had been the same person that had been "coughing" during the conference session. As it turns out, this woman was completely set free from the demonic spirit that tormented her. This is the freedom that Jesus Christ brings! Later on in the book I will relate another (but not the only) more direct experience of victory and the authority of the name of Jesus.

While the thought that even Christians experience struggles with demons is a little controversial, the main source of this confusion comes from a misunderstanding of what is commonly called "possession". The biblical term transliterated *"daimonizomai"* commonly translated as "demon-possessed" means most simply "under the influence of demons" to one extent or another.[1] This influence can range from:

- The suggestion of simple thoughts and thought patterns planted by the enemy. This type of struggle is common to all, and is symptomatic of the ongoing warfare we all face. We manage this ongoing warfare by taking thoughts captive to the authority of God's word. (2 Corinthians 10:4,5; Matthew 4:1-11; Luke 4:1-13) Resisting the devil so he flees (James 4:7) And renewing of the mind with Holy Scripture. (Romans 12:2).
- Demonic influence can be the underlying cause of physical maladies (Luke 13:10-17, Matthew 9:33, 10:8); the answer – cast out the demon in the authority of the name of Jesus while praying for God's healing touch.
- "*Daimonizomai*" can describe the complete control by demonic forces of aspects of a person's personality. The person has lost or has not given Christ control of the area being subjugated to demonic influence.

(Luke 8:26-39) The answer – surrender the area to Christ and cast the demon(s) out.

Let me take a moment to state that throughout this book we will be sharing what the Holy Bible - God's Word, has to say about the subject of demonic influence and Christ's victory. We will be using a few different translations to help clarify certain passages, and using **bold** type to help emphasize certain words and passages. I will also use square brackets [] to encapsulate explanatory comments and definitions. A few scriptural examples of Jesus delivering people from demonic strongholds are Matthew 4:24 and 8:16. Read, "under demonic influence" where the translators use "demon-possessed":

*"Then His [Jesus] fame went throughout all Syria; and they brought to Him all **sick people** who were **afflicted** with various **diseases** and **torments**, and those who were **demon-possessed**, **epileptics**, and **paralytics**; and **He healed them**."*
Matthew 4:24, NKJV

Notice in the verse above the kinds of issues Jesus is prepared to deal with:
1. Sick people afflicted with:
   a. Various Diseases
   b. Torments
2. Those under the influence of demons
3. Epileptics
4. Paralytics

And HE HEALED THEM!

*"That evening many demon-possessed people were brought to Jesus. All **the spirits fled when he commanded them to leave**; and **he healed all the sick**."*
Matthew 8:16, NLT

Fortunately for us, Jesus' sacrifice on the cross and resurrection from the dead has provided the means for us to be set free from these wicked forces and healed of the inflictions and torments they have brought upon us!

*"...always thanking the Father, who has enabled you to share the inheritance that belongs to God's holy people, who live in the light. For **he has rescued us from the one who***

rules in the kingdom of darkness, and he has brought us into the Kingdom of his dear Son. *God has purchased our freedom with his blood and has forgiven all our sins."*
Colossians 1:12-14, NLT

    Satan's agents, aka *demons* and fallen angels, often hide in order to maintain their stronghold. They can be holding on even after one comes to Christ. This demonic activity is identified in scripture as a *"stronghold".* (2 Corinthians 10:4) These *strongholds* are demonic fortifications if you will, built in areas of our minds and personalities darkened by Satan's lies. The key is to allow the Holy Spirit through the word of God to expose them and deal with them. Pull them down! *"Resist the Devil, and he will flee from you."* (James 4:7)

    Throughout the course of my walk with Jesus, the Lord has used me to help others be set free from the power of the enemy through prayer to God, and confrontation of the enemy in the authority of Jesus name. I know first hand that the name of Jesus is the name above all names, and every knee bows to Him. Demons especially are no exception, so read on in hopeful anticipation of your own deliverance, **or in the very least, gain an understanding of how you can be a help to others with the understanding gleaned from Holy Scripture.**

*"Your attitude should be the same that Christ Jesus had. Though he was God, he did not demand and cling to his rights as God. He made himself nothing; he took the humble position of a slave and appeared in human form. And in human form **he obediently humbled himself** even further by dying a criminal's death on a cross. Because of this, **God raised him up to the heights of heaven and gave him a name that is above every other name, so that at the name of Jesus every knee will bow, in heaven** and **on earth** and **under the earth**, and every tongue will confess that Jesus Christ is Lord, to the glory of God the Father."*
Philippians 2:5-11, NLT

What great news, that at the name of Jesus:

EVERY knee shall bow! Christ's humility resulted in exultation, and our humility before

Christ's will result in deliverance. Every knee shall bow:

In heaven - angels and every spiritual being in heaven is subject to Christ, planets, stars, all seen and unseen elements of the cosmos, biological or inter-dimensional
On earth - men, women, animals, the planet, its atmosphere, oceans, microbes, any spiritual being banished to this planetary sphere
Under the earth – All the realm of the great abyss, all demons, wicked angelic beings, denizens of hell and the grave

Over all **JESUS CHRIST IS LORD**!

My prayer is that as I share the following ten scriptural principles of deliverance, you engage with God as His very words are delivered to you. May His word sink deep into your heart, may you understand with your mind, believe in your heart, and may you be completely set free from all that Satan has brought against you through the grace and love of Jesus the Messiah.
Amen!

Principle One: GOD LOVES YOU!

    Are you inflicted with unexplainable illness, addictions, or compulsions? Have you been to the doctor for that unidentified condition, but come up empty? You tried to quit that annoying and/or destructive habit more times than you can count, but keep going back for more. This book is for you, and good news awaits you! There may be more at work than just physical disease or your personal failings. It may be that evil spirits (unseen malevolent beings) are tormenting, manipulating, and overall causing you ill. **Do not despair, God, the Creator of the universe loves you and can set you free. Better still, He wants to set you free!**

Let me state from the outset, I am not trying to propose a substitute for trained medical attention, nor a replacement for sound counseling. Nor do I pretend that this is a complete treatment of the subject. What I do propose is that all true healing comes from God, including the natural processes He built into our minds and bodies, the insights provided through scientific research, and His direct intervention beyond the natural process.

Disease can be caused by the natural disruption of a fallen biological order (germs, cellular mutations, viruses, hostile bacteria, age, physical injury, etc.), or, as revealed in the Bible yet often hard to distinguish from the former, by intervention of forces beyond nature, know in the Bible as "demons" who are under the command of Satan, also know as the Devil and Lucifer.

In addition, "psychosomatic" disorders - physical symptoms caused by disturbed mental states and stress, are well documented.[2] Sometimes the best trained doctors, psychologists, psychiatrists, and therapists miss or dismiss the *spiritual* roots of some of our maladies. So while we do not suggest abandoning any treatment you may currently be receiving, we are inviting you to explore some vital information contained in the ancient yet surprisingly relevant and authoritative text of the Holy Bible, information your enemies don't want you know!

The Holy Spirit put this book on my heart for you! God wants to do 4 things for you…

1) God wants you to know how much He loves you!
2) God the Father wants you to know that He sent Jesus to die on the cross to forgive you and cleanse you from all your sins; things we have done wrong that violate God's moral principles and demands. (see a fuller treatment in the Glossary at the end of the book)
3) God wants to heal you of past wounds caused by the sins of others
4) God wants to set you free from **ALL** the power of the Devil; the chief evildoer and enemy of your soul. As a matter of fact, He has already set you free through the work of Christ on the cross, you just need to

make that victory your own by coming into agreement with what God has done.

Listen to what the Bible says...

Forgiveness of sins and deliverance from the powers of darkness is offered in Christ

"...giving thanks to the Father who has qualified us to be partakers of the inheritance of the saints in the light. ***He has delivered us from the power of darkness*** *and conveyed us into the kingdom of the Son of His love, in whom* ***we have redemption through His blood, the forgiveness of sins****. He is the image of the invisible God, the firstborn over all creation."*
Colossians 1:12-15, NKJV

Notice, God "has" delivered us, it is already done, and we "have" redemption and forgiveness of sins through the blood of God's Son Jesus. This is yours today if you will but receive it! You can enter into Christ's kingdom as you enter into Him by faith.

Set free from Satan's power

"For this purpose the Son of God was manifested [made known, appear]*, that he* [Jesus] *might destroy the works of the devil."*
1 John 3:8b, KJV

The American Heritage Dictionary defines "deliver" as "to release or rescue; set free: *deliver one from slavery.*" So "deliverance" is "the act of delivering," and "the condition of being delivered, especially from bondage or danger."[3] **The purpose of this book is to give you the information you need to be DELIVERED and set free from the bondage of sin and Satan.**

We are not going to explore every nuance of interpretation, or argue every point where there may be disagreement in the believing Christian community or other religions regarding the matter of deliverance from evil spirits. What we will do is outline the fundamental problem as revealed in God's Word - the Bible, name the enemy, and deal with the enemy using the tools God has given us; the Word of God, the blood of Jesus, prayer, and faith filled proclamation.

A few last comments before we move on. 1) God loves you whoever you are, whatever your background, even un-churched or non-Christian. **YOU can be set free by the love, forgiveness, and power of God,** but you have to meet His conditions to be set free. The following pages outline humanities problem and the provision God has made to set you free. I will try to define terms in the body of the text, but if you are unfamiliar with certain words, I have included a glossary in the back of the book, and any good English dictionary can help with ones I may have missed.

2) Sometimes deliverance and healing come all at once, while other times it is a process as our minds become renewed and weeds become exposed in the garden of our hearts. Think of this book as a tool intended to point you to God's heavenly compass or GPS, the Bible. When you are in unknown territory, if you have your compass or GPS, (the Bible and faith), you can find your way. Sound, faith based Christian counseling, godly friendships and fellowship with other believers, and ongoing teaching from God's word will help reassure your liberty in Christ. We are in a

battle, and we need one another as we wage warfare against our common spiritual enemy.

Principal Two: Understand the Big Mess

Nearly 2000 years ago, when Jesus came preaching the gospel - the good news of the Kingdom of God, he did not appear in a time vacuum, so a basic understanding of the facts requires some historical context. According to the Bible, by the time Jesus was incarnate (*incarnate* - a pre-existent being entering into the complete life cycle of humanity, becoming flesh and blood) in the womb of the Virgin Mary (Luke 1:26-38), there were at least 4000 years of human history since the creation and fall of Adam and Eve.

There is an eternity in the realm of Yahweh (God's personal name in the Hebrew language of the Old Testament, see entry in the Glossary at the back of the book) the Triune God, and unknown epochs in the created realm of the heavenly beings by the time Christ (the promised Messiah, one anointed to rule and reign) came. In Yahweh's eternal plan he prepared a special people, Israel, in a special place, the land of Canaan, now known as the land of Israel after the people to whom he promised it, in order to do his special work, liberate not just Israel or the Jews, but all humanity from the terrible mess they were in; bondage to sin and subservience to the kingdom of darkness.

Faith - A Core Principle

Completely understanding the mess we humans find ourselves in first requires an acceptance of the fact that "we are not alone" in the universe, and I am not talking about biological space aliens. One, our Creator, the maker of heaven, earth, and all that exists, God Almighty the Triune Yahweh, is ever present through His Spirit, and two, there are an innumerable number of other unseen created beings of various types in a different dimension, many of which were created before mankind. It is important to highlight that accepting the truth of God's existence and authority is key to your deliverance:

"So, you see, it is impossible to please God without faith. Anyone who wants to come to him must believe that there is a God and that he rewards those who sincerely seek him."
Hebrews 11:6, NLT

The LORD also made this promise:

"And ye shall seek me, and find me, when ye shall search for me with all your heart."
Jeremiah 29:13, KJV

God's promise to you is if you will seek Him with all your heart, you will find Him. Believe that He is, and that he will reward you if you seek Him out. More than that, it is God himself who is drawing you toward him by his Holy Spirit. My prayer is that this book in your hand provides you the opportunity to yield to God's loving call.

When God created human beings (Hebrew = *adam*, or children of *adam* in the Bible), men and women, he made them in His own *"image and likeness"*. So "adam" refers to both the human race - mankind, and the personal name of the first man (male).

*"And God said, Let us make man [adam] in our **image**, after our **likeness**: and let **them** have **dominion** over the fish of the sea, and over the fowl of the air, and over the cattle, and over all the earth, and over every creeping thing that creepeth upon the earth. **So God created man** [adam] **in his own image, in the image of God created he him; <u>male and female created he them.</u>"***
Genesis 1:26, 27, KJV

Adam and Eve, the first man and woman, shared some of Yahweh's appearance (image), and some of His personal characteristics (likeness), making humans unique among the created beings. God performed this wonderful act in the presence of the myriad of heavenly beings as He stated to His servant Job:

*"Then the LORD answered Job from the whirlwind: "Who is this that questions my wisdom with such ignorant words? Brace yourself, because I have some questions for you, and you must answer them. "Where were you when I laid the foundations of the earth? Tell me, if you know so much. Do you know how its dimensions were determined and who did the surveying? What supports its foundations, and who laid its cornerstone **as the morning stars sang together and all the angels shouted for joy?**"*
Job 38:1-7, NLT

    God then gave Adam and Eve dominion as stewards over all of the earth, while some of the angels had continued responsibility in maintaining the material order of the cosmos.

    Two problems occurred which caused the mess we find ourselves in. One, some of the heavenly beings started sedition against God, the Bible indicates about a third (Revelation 12:4,9). Two, the leader of the sedition in heaven, Satan (meaning *adversary* in Hebrew), through lies and deception caused Adam and Eve to sin against God. When they fell they corrupted the divine image, and became subject to death and the manipulations of the fallen heavenly beings, even though they were intended to be sovereign on the earth under God. Satan, the old serpent, usurped Adam and Eve's God given authority on the earth and in so doing he attempted (unsuccessfully of course) to usurp Yahweh's authority as well. When Satan enticed them to sin - violate God's command, the condition of sin and subservience was passed to all their decedents. Adam and Eve had surrendered their authority when they disobeyed God, and gave into Satan's temptation and the lusts of their own hearts.

Let me take a moment to make very clear, the contributions of the "prince of the power of the air" (another descriptor for Satan, Ephesian 2:2), does not remove the culpability - personal guilt and responsibility of Adam and Eve. They knew God's word, yet still choose to not trust and obey their loving Creator, but rather trust the words of a deceitful spirit! Satan's tricks do not remove our own culpability in this day and age either.

The good news is that through the work of Jesus on the cross, all humanity has been given a chance to reverse the poor

decision made by Adam and Eve, and the poor decisions we make personally, we can put our trust in God by obedience to the gospel – the Good News, more on this later. (In case you haven't noticed, we are trying to emphasize that the word *gospel* means *good news!*)

Principle Three: Understand the Enemy

God's one Request to Adam and Eve and the consequence for breaking it:

"And the LORD God took the man, and put him into the garden of Eden to dress it and to keep it. And the LORD God commanded the man, saying, Of every tree of the garden thou mayest freely eat: ***But of the tree of the knowledge of good and evil, thou shalt not eat of it: for in the day that thou eatest thereof thou shalt surely die.****"*
Genesis 2:15-17, KJV

Deceiver:

"Now the serpent [Hebrew *Nachash*: serpent, enchanter] *was more cunning than any beast of the field which the LORD God had made. And he said to the woman, "Has God indeed said, 'You shall not eat of every tree of the garden'?" And the woman said to the serpent, "We may eat the fruit of the trees of the garden; "but of the fruit of the tree which is in the midst of the garden, God has said, 'You shall not eat it, nor shall you touch it, lest you die.'" Then the serpent said to the woman, "You will not surely die. "For God knows that in the day you eat of it your eyes will be opened, and you will be like God, knowing good and evil."*

"So when the woman saw that the tree was good for food, that it was pleasant to the eyes, and a tree desirable to make one wise, she took of its fruit and ate. She also gave to her husband with her, and he ate. Then the eyes of both of them were opened, and they knew that they were naked; and they sewed fig leaves together and made themselves coverings. And they heard the sound of the LORD God walking in the garden in the cool of the day, and Adam

and his wife hid themselves from the presence of the LORD God among the trees of the garden." Genesis 3:1-8, NKJV

While there is much to consider in the passage above, three facts are readily observed:

1) Satan, *the serpent*, in his craftiness gets Eve to overthink God's command, which simply was not to eat from *the tree of the knowledge of good and evil* in the center of the garden, or the process of death will begin and they will die. Adam, also well aware of the command, rather than intervene in the exchange, rebelliously went along with his wife and the serpent, for he was "*with her*". Regarding *death*, the Hebrew literally says "dying you shall die":[4] immediate spiritual death, progressive degradation of the mind, and ultimately death of the body.

2) Adam and Eve failed to allow their God given natural desires for flavorful food, beauty, and wisdom, to be governed by

God's loving direction. His one command, "eat from everything but this one tree, for if you do eat this one, you will die". They had freedom, and were given authority over the entire earth and all creatures on it, and muffed it for that one fruit. How often have we surrendered our own greater good and freedoms in the same way? "If I could only ____ (fill in the blank) just once" **This is the ultimate nature of sin, letting our own natural desires govern our lives contrary to what is "good".** Desires that are not bad in and of themselves become twisted and corrupted by sin.

3) Like little children who hide when they realize they have disobeyed their parents, Adam and Eve hid, and tried to cover their shame. This is also exactly what we do. In addition, I can almost hear the serpent rubbing it in and shouting as God approached: "Oops Adam and Eve, you really messed up

now, better run and hide before God catches you"!

Enemy:

What is very interesting as you read the rest of the story for yourself, is that God does not shout at Adam and Eve, nor condemn them (after all, he was planning on taking a walk with them), but instead draws out their confession, and outlines the severity of the consequences for their actions. **God makes it clear the "serpent" aka Satan is their enemy**. God then promises ultimate redemption and defeat of the enemy through a future offspring, the "seed" of the woman. **This illustrates that Yahweh is truly a loving heavenly Father, and has a greater plan that we can often comprehend.**

"So the LORD God said to the serpent, "Because you have done this, you will be punished. You are singled out from all the domestic and wild animals of the whole earth to be cursed. You will grovel in the dust as long as you live, crawling along on your belly. From now on, you and the woman will be enemies, and

your offspring and her offspring will be enemies. He will crush your head, and you will strike his heel."''
Genesis 3:14, 15, NLT.

Principle Four: Understand Sins Consequence

"Wherefore, as by one man sin entered into the world, and death by sin; ***and so death passed upon all men,*** [all humanity] *for that all have sinned:"*
Romans 5:12, KJV

Because Adam was the first human, he was representative for the entire race because all humanity would stem from *them* (Adam and Eve – the mother of all living). Unfortunate decisions have unfortunate consequences, and all humanity inherits the consequence of death, because we all have participated in Adams transgression *"in Adam"*. In other words, we were genetically inside Adam and Eve when they sinned, and the corruption of that act passes on to us, each of us having the propensity toward sin, and each acting out this inclination in his or her own life. **The good news is we can create a new association through a new representative, that is Jesus the Messiah.**

*"For since by man came death, by Man also came the resurrection of the dead. For as **in Adam** all die, even so **in Christ all shall be made alive**."*
1 Corinthians 15:21-22, NKJV

Christ died for all humanity, but the benefits can only be realized through putting complete faith in what he has accomplished through His death on the cross, his burial, and resurrection on the third day:

*"For therefore we both labour and suffer reproach, because we trust in the living God, who is **the Saviour of all men, specially of those that believe**."*
1 Timothy 4:10, KJV

"Moreover, brethren, I declare to you the gospel which I preached to you ... that Christ

died for our sins according to the Scriptures, and that He was buried, and that He rose again the third day according to the Scriptures, and that He was seen...."
1 Corinthians 15:1-5, NKJV

So death; physical, mental, and spiritual or said another way - death in body, soul, and spirit, is the consequence of sin on all humanity. But, the gracious gift of God is eternal life to those who put their trust in Him through the gospel.

"For the wages of sin is death; but the gift of God is eternal life through Jesus Christ our Lord."
Romans 6:23, KJV

Principle Five: Understand the Holy Angels

In order to make sure we remove all ambiguity as to the identity of the "serpent" in the Genesis passages, lets look at a few verses contained in the prophesy Jesus gave to the apostle John, widely known as the book of *Revelation* or *The Apocalypse*, the last book in the New Testament.

*"And **the great dragon** was cast out, that **old serpent, called the Devil, and Satan**, which **deceiveth** the whole world: he was cast out into the earth, and his angels were cast out with him."*
Revelation 12:9, KJV

*"And he laid hold on the dragon, that **old serpent, which is the Devil, and Satan**, and bound him a thousand years..."*
Revelation 20:2, KJV

These passages from the book of Revelation make it quite evident that the serpent identified in the Garden of Eden is one and the same with:

1) The great dragon
2) Satan
3) Devil
4) Deceiver

We will also discover that listening to Satan was not the best idea humanity ever had. Some things never change, and people are still doing it. The enemy is very seductive, especially when combined with our own natural desires twisted by sin. Satan's schemes and human desire twisted by sin, this combination is deadly.

I want to take this opportunity to say that while the enemy of our soul is ancient and powerful, and has drawn quite a following both from heaven and on earth, he is not an equal with Yahweh (the true Creator), but a created being along with us. In addition, **Satan's rebel angelic forces are still out numbered 2 to 1 by the heavenly host** (the word translated "host" in the Bible means "army") loyal to God. The Bible indicates that the Devil only drew 1/3rd with him, and in the end Michael the archangel (*archangel* means head or governing angel) and his army kicks them out.

*"And there appeared another wonder in heaven; and behold a great red dragon, having seven heads and ten horns, and seven crowns upon his heads. And his tail drew **the third part of the stars of heaven*** [often in the Bible, and in the book of Revelation in particular, "stars" often represent angels, Rev 1:20b], *and did cast them to the earth...And there was war in heaven: Michael and his angels fought against the dragon; and the dragon fought and his angels, And prevailed not; neither was their place found any more in heaven. **And the great dragon was cast out, that old serpent, called the Devil, and Satan, which deceiveth the***

whole world: he was cast out into the earth, and his angels were cast out with him."
Revelation 12:3,7-9, KJV.

The Holy Angels

So we can see, God's holy angels outnumber the Satan's wicked angels 2 to 1.

What is an "Angel"?

If one were to ask what an angel is, we could very simply answer, "a messenger of God". That is what the word "angel" means in Greek, the original language of the New Testament. In fact "angel" in English is an Anglicized from the Greek "*angelos*".

In Hebrew, the original language of what Jewish people call the Tenach and Christians call the Old Testament or Hebrew Scriptures, the word "*malach*" also translated "*angel*" in English, means the same thing, a messenger or ambassador. What do we most often find angels doing in the Bible as it relates to humans? Bringing messages from God! But they do much more than that; the holy angels do God's bidding on the earth and heaven, make up His army - His "heavenly host", take

Yahweh's direction in sustaining the cosmos, implement God's judgments, and my personal favorite, **act as guardians to God's faithful chosen people on earth**.

*"And God never said to an angel, as he did to his Son [Jesus], "Sit in honor at my right hand until I humble your enemies, making them a footstool under your feet." **But angels are only servants. They are spirits sent from God to care for those who will receive salvation."** Hebrews 1:13, 14, NLT*

The primary distinction between Satan and his minions and the angels of God is God's angels act out of pure devotion and obedience to Yahweh the Creator, while Satan's hordes are always willing to interject themselves toward anyone willing to pay them heed. While they are still messengers, they are messengers of lies and deception! However, God is able to bring His purposes about, in spite of a rebellious horde of fallen spirits and humanity.

*"For you are the children of your father **the Devil**, and you love to do the evil things he*

*does. **He was a murderer from the beginning** and has always hated the truth. There is no truth in him. When he lies, it is consistent with his character; **for he is a liar and the father of lies**."*
John 8:44, NLT

The Devil-Satan-serpent does evil things, was a murderer from the beginning, hates the truth, has no truth in him, lies and is the father of lies. Contrast this to Jesus who compared Himself to the good shepherd and the gate to the sheep, while the Devil and those who would teach salvation outside of Jesus are thieves and robbers:

*"... so he explained it to them. "I assure you, I am the gate for the sheep," he said. "All others who came before me were thieves and robbers. But the true sheep did not listen to them. **Yes, I am the gate. Those who come in through me will be saved**. Wherever they go, they will find green pastures. **The thief's purpose is to steal and kill and destroy**. My purpose is to give life in all its fullness. "I am the good shepherd. The good shepherd lays down his life for the sheep." John 10:7-11, NLT.*

Contrast the desires of the heavenly angels with Satan's.

God's angels don't seek worship, but rather worship God:

*"I, John, am the one who saw and heard all these things. And when I saw and heard these things, **I fell down to worship the angel who showed them to me. But again he said, "No, don't worship me. I am a servant of God, just like you** and your brothers the prophets, as well as all who obey what is written in this scroll. **Worship God!""***
Revelation 22:8, 9, NLT

Lets consider the angels from the story most hear at Christmas time, the wonderful announcement to the shepherds:

*"That night some shepherds were in the fields outside the village, guarding their flocks of sheep. Suddenly, **an angel of the Lord appeared** among them, and the radiance of the Lord's glory surrounded them. They were terribly frightened, but the angel reassured them. "Don't be afraid!" he said. "I bring you*

good news of great joy for everyone! **The Savior--yes, the Messiah, the Lord--has been born tonight in Bethlehem, the city of David!** *And this is how you will recognize him: You will find a baby lying in a manger, wrapped snugly in strips of cloth!"* **Suddenly, the angel was joined by a vast host of others--the armies of heaven--praising God: "Glory to God in the highest heaven, and peace on earth to all whom God favors.""**
Luke 2:8-14, NLT

The above story is just one of the many passages that reveal how God's holy angels love to sing, praise, and worship Him. They are often reflected as joining in when humans praise and worship God. (Psalm 103:20, 148:2, Hebrews 12:22, Revelation 5:11, 7:11)

The Devil and his "angels" are opposed to God, His purposes, and His people. Satan is still looking for people who will worship him and take his direction in opposition to God. He even tried to get Jesus to do it!

"Then Jesus, full of the Holy Spirit, left the Jordan River. He was led by the Spirit to go out

into the wilderness, where the Devil tempted him for forty days. He ate nothing all that time and was very hungry. Then the Devil said to him, "If you are the Son of God, change this stone into a loaf of bread." But Jesus told him, "No! The Scriptures say, 'People need more than bread for their life.'" Then the Devil took him up and revealed to him all the kingdoms of the world in a moment of time. The Devil told him, "I will give you the glory of these kingdoms and authority over them--because they are mine to give to anyone I please. I will give it all to you if you will bow down and worship me." Jesus replied, "The Scriptures say, 'You must worship the Lord your God; serve only him.'"
Luke 4:1-8, NLT

The key to defeating Satan is to follow Jesus' example, knowing the scripture, which is "the sword of the Spirit" (Ephesians 6:17), knowing how to use it, and knowing when it is being misused. As we have already seen, Satan is skilled at twisting and misdirecting by using God's word out of context and apart from God's intended meaning. Jesus, as the last "Adam", our new representative, contrary to Adam and Eve, properly resisted Satan's deceptions and stood firm on the revealed will of the heavenly Father. Through faith, Christ's obedience can become our obedience, and your key to deliverance!

Principle Six: Understand God's Promise

We mentioned earlier that the Lord promised at the time of the fall of Adam and Eve to one day restore man's place and defeat the serpent through the promised "seed" of the woman. This promise was fulfilled when God the Son (Colossians 1:9-29) took upon Himself the seed of David of the Israelite tribe of Judah, became incarnate in the womb of a virgin named Mary, and was born in Bethlehem, a town in the land of Israel a few miles from Jerusalem, just like the prophet Micah foretold:

"But you, Bethlehem Ephrathah, Though you are little among the thousands of Judah, Yet

out of you shall come forth to Me The One to be Ruler in Israel, Whose goings forth are from of old, From everlasting."
Micah 5:2, NKJV

The Promise – a messiah, "the seed" will come to totally vanquish the "serpent"

"So the LORD God said to the serpent: "Because you have done this, You are cursed more than all cattle, And more than every beast of the field; On your belly you shall go, And you shall eat dust All the days of your life. ***And I will put enmity between you and the woman, And between your seed and her Seed; He shall bruise your head, And you shall bruise His heel.""***
Genesis 3:14, 15, NKJV

And the prophets continue to declare the promise:

"Therefore the Lord himself shall give you a sign; Behold, a virgin shall conceive, and bear a son, and shall call his name Immanuel."
Isaiah 7:14, KJV see also Matthew 1:23
[*Immanuel* means "God with us"]

Approximately 4000 years after God made the promise to Adam and Eve, the one came who would ultimately step on (bruise) the serpent's head. Even while the process of defeating the serpent caused suffering to Jesus (bruised his heal), Jesus gained the victory through the cross. **Fellow humans, we are at war with the forces of darkness and we can be victorious only if we surrender ourselves to the true victor, Jesus.**

The Fulfillment – Jesus the Messiah is born:

*"Now in the sixth month the angel Gabriel was sent by God to a city of Galilee named Nazareth, to a virgin betrothed to a man whose name was Joseph, of the house of David. The virgin's name was Mary. And having come in, the angel said to her, "Rejoice, highly favored one, the Lord is with you; blessed are you among women!" But when she saw him, she was troubled at his saying, and considered what manner of greeting this was. Then the angel said to her, "Do not be afraid, Mary, for you have found favor with God. "And behold, **you will conceive in your womb and bring forth a***

Son, and shall call His name JESUS. "He will be great, and will be called the Son of the Highest; and the Lord God will give Him the throne of His father David. "And He will reign over the house of Jacob forever, and of His kingdom there will be no end." *Then Mary said to the angel, "How can this be, since I do not know a man?" And the angel answered and said to her, "The Holy Spirit will come upon you, and the power of the Highest will overshadow you; therefore, also,* ***that Holy One who is to be born will be called the Son of God."***
Luke 1:26-35, NKJV

And the angel spoke to Joseph:

"But while he thought on these things, behold, the angel of the Lord appeared unto him in a dream, saying, Joseph, thou son of David, fear not to take unto thee Mary thy wife: for that which is conceived in her is of the Holy Ghost. ***And she shall bring forth a son, and thou shalt call his name JESUS: for he shall save his people from their sins."***
Matthew 1:20, 21, KJV

Jesus, the seed of the daughter of Eve, is given the "thrown of David" to be king over God's people, with everlasting dominion as King of kings and Lord of lords! The name *Jesus* is the Anglicized form of the Greek Ιησους - *Iesous,* a transliteration the Hebrew word "*Yeshua*" - ישוע, which literally means, "Salvation or Yahweh is Salvation". We will discuss this a bit more later and in the glossary. Suffice it to say, Jesus came to "*save his people from their sins*", and He was named appropriately, it was no accident.

Principle Two Continued: Downward Trend

Lets return to the subject of the big mess caused by the fall of humanity into sin. After the fall of Adam, things went from bad to worse as sins foothold became stronger. It even came to the point that some of the "sons of God" (angelic beings created directly by God) left their "realm", "dimension", or what Jude (or *Judah*), Jesus' brother called their "own habitation" (Jude 6), and entered into rebellious relations with human women. Rather than resist this encroachment on their domain, just as they had listened to the serpent-Satan in Eden, the human population came to accept this tyranny with willing participation, so God determined to destroy the earth with a great flood.[5]

These events became mythologized in various forms across many cultures of the ancient world; there is hardly a culture that does not have both a flood tradition, and a tradition of heavenly beings intermixing with humans. The Holy Sprit through Moses stripped the mythical and superfluous elements out of the Holy Scriptures, leaving us the necessary information to know the gist of the matter; **humanity was in complete rebellion against their Creator,** and instead of subjecting themselves to Yahweh, had subjected themselves to fallen angelic usurpers and their own vain imaginations. **They served the creature rather than the creator**.

This corruption was not isolated to angel and man, but through them the corruption even spread to other earthly creatures that became victims of their depravity.

*"So God looked upon the earth, and indeed it was corrupt; for **all flesh had***

corrupted their way on the earth. *And God said to Noah, "The end of all flesh has come before Me, for* **the earth is filled with violence through them**; *and behold, I will destroy them with the earth."*
Genesis 6:12, 13, NKJV

Thank God for his grace toward our very great grandfather Noah! It took great courage and faith for Noah to act against the tide of all society at the time, and instead obey the voice of his Creator.

In the time of Noah before the flood, humanity continued to corrupt itself with the malevolent fallen beings:

"And Noah was five hundred years old: and Noah begat Shem, Ham, and Japheth.
And it came to pass, when men began to multiply on the face of the earth, and daughters were born unto them, That the sons of God saw the daughters of men that they were fair; and they took them wives of all which they chose. And the LORD said, My spirit shall not always strive with man, for that he also is flesh: yet his days shall be an hundred and twenty years.

There were giants [Hebrew=Nephelim] *in the earth in those days; and also after that, when the sons of God came in unto the daughters of men, and they bare children to them, the same became mighty men which were of old, men of renown.*

And GOD saw that the wickedness of man was great in the earth, and that every imagination of the thoughts of his heart was only evil continually. *And it repented the LORD that he had made man on the earth, and **it grieved him at his heart**. And the LORD said, I will destroy man whom I have created from the face of the earth; both man, and beast, and the creeping thing, and the fowls of the air; for it repenteth me that I have made them. But Noah found grace in the eyes of the LORD."*
Genesis 5:32-6:8, KJV

While often depicted as a nice children's story, the reality behind the salvation on the ark is a completely perverse and corrupted humanity that had subjected themselves to wholly corrupted spiritual forces. Only God's grace and favor toward one man of faith, his immediate family, and the animals brought onto the ark, saved life on the earth at that time. Of special interest, and disturbance, is Jesus said that when he returns, it would be like the days of Noah again (Luke 17:26-27).

The rebellious progeny of the seditious angels and their human mates that were destroyed in the flood became, according to accepted Jewish tradition at the time of Jesus, disembodied evil spirits or demons, that are cursed to roam the atmospheric surface of the earth until final judgment, and they are always looking for footholds into another body.[6] (Matthew 8:28-34) The specific seditious angels from the pre-flood days that left their appointed positions to co-mingle with humanity are locked in a dark abyss. (2 Peter 2:4-6, Jude 6)

*"For if **God did not spare the angels who sinned, but cast them down to hell and delivered them into chains of darkness, to be reserved for judgment;** and did not spare the ancient world, but saved Noah, one of eight people, a preacher of righteousness, bringing in the flood on the world of the ungodly;"*
2 Peter 2:4, 5, NKJV

*"I will therefore put you in remembrance, though ye once knew this, how that the Lord, having saved the people out of the land of Egypt, afterward destroyed them that believed not. **And the angels which kept not their first estate, but left their own habitation, he hath reserved in everlasting chains under darkness unto the judgment of the great day.** Even as Sodom and Gomorrha, and the cities about them in like manner, giving themselves over to fornication, and going after strange flesh, are set forth for an example, suffering the vengeance of eternal fire."*
Jude 1:5-7, KJV

After the flood, God began to work with humans by establishing covenants - agreements and promises between two parties, with stipulations of the consequences when a party violates the agreement. In addition, God made promises. **The fact that Yahweh keeps these covenants and promises recorded in the Bible establishes objective evidence that He truly is GOD**, particularly in regard to the people of Israel and the New Covenant Body of Christ. **He keeps covenant and fulfills HIS promises.**

"Know therefore that the LORD thy God, he is God, the faithful God, which keepeth covenant and mercy with them that love him and keep his commandments to a thousand generations;"
Deuteronomy 7:9, KJV

He made a covenant promise with all earthly creation after the flood that he would not destroy the entire earth with water ever again, and gave the rainbow as a sign (Genesis 9:8-17). The fulfillment of this covenant on Yahweh's part is exact; there has not been a global flood since Noah's time. It is unfortunate that perverse militant political groups seeking to reestablish elements of the pre-flood depravity are using the very sign God gave as a symbol of His covenant of peace, the rainbow, as symbolic of their movement.

*"**And God spake unto Noah, and to his sons with him, saying, And I, behold, I establish my covenant with you, and with your seed after you; And with every living**"*

*creature that is with you, of the fowl, of the cattle, and of every beast of the earth with you; from all that go out of the ark, to every beast of the earth. And **I will establish my covenant with you; neither shall all flesh be cut off any more by the waters of a flood**; neither shall there any more be a flood to destroy the earth. And God said, **This is the token of the covenant which I make between me and you and every living creature that is with you, for perpetual generations: I do set my bow [rainbow] in the cloud, and it shall be for a token of a covenant between me and the earth**. And it shall come to pass, when I bring a cloud over the earth, that the bow shall be seen in the cloud: And I will remember my covenant, which is between me and you and every living creature of all flesh; and the waters shall no more become a flood to destroy all flesh. And the bow shall be in the cloud; and I will look upon it, that I may remember the everlasting covenant between God and every living creature of all flesh that is upon the earth. **And God said unto Noah, This is the token of the covenant, which I have established between me and all flesh that is upon the earth**." Genesis 9:8-17, KJV*

The blessed God made a covenant with all creatures on the earth not to destroy the earth with a flood ever again, and the rainbow is His sign that that He will fulfill this promise.

The primary covenant of the Old Testament and to which most subsequent ones refer back to was the covenant God made with Abraham regarding his "seed" being blessed, a blessing, and inheriting the land of Canaan. (Genesis 12:1-3, 15:1-21, 17:1-22, 22:15-19) God re-confirmed the covenant with Isaac (Genesis 26:24), and Jacob whose name was changed to Israel (Genesis 28:10-15, 32:24-30), with all Israel (Exodus 19-20 et al), and with David (2 Samuel 7:1-17) in terms of the royal line through whom would come the Messiah.

The consummate blessing of the *seed* of Abraham was Christ, the promised *seed* of the woman, the *seed* of David, the Son of God. God's promises to Israel were fulfilled, as were the consequences for not keeping the covenant with God, exile from the land of promise (Daniel 9:11, Jeremiah 25:12), and God's promise to bring them back to the land, not once, but twice. They returned to the land 70 years after the Babylonian began exile precisely as God had predicted in Jeremiah 25:12, and they have been gathered from the nearly 2000 year Roman diaspora from all over the earth just as God had predicted through the prophets. (Deuteronomy 30:1-10, Jeremiah 16:14, Psalm 126, Isaiah 11:11,12) The Isaiah passage is quite significant; because it mentions both the "second" gathering of Israel from the nations, the "ensign" (flag, banner), clearly a messianic prediction, and that Jews and Gentiles (non Jews) would also seek out the Messiah.

*"And in that day there shall be a **root of Jesse, which shall stand for an ensign of the people; to it shall the Gentiles seek**: and his rest shall be glorious. And it shall come to pass in that day, that **the Lord shall set his hand again the second time to recover the remnant of his people**, which shall be left, from Assyria, and from Egypt, and from Pathros, and from Cush, and from Elam, and from Shinar, and from Hamath, and from the islands of the sea. **And he shall set up an ensign for the nations, and shall assemble the outcasts of Israel,***

and gather together the dispersed of Judah from the four corners of the earth."
Isaiah 11:10-12, KJV

In the very next paragraph it is made clear who this root of Jesse, the ensign for the people is:

*"And in that day you will say: "O LORD, I will praise You; Though You were angry with me, Your anger is turned away, and You comfort me. Behold, **God is my salvation**, I will trust and not be afraid; '**For YAH, the LORD**, is my strength and song; **He also has become my salvation**.'" Therefore with joy you will **draw water from the wells of salvation**."*
Isaiah 12:1-3, NKJV

As we have learned already, *Jesus* is derived from the Hebrew word *Yeshua*, and that is the exact Hebrew word used in the above passage. Drink from the well of God's salvation by putting your faith and trust in the Messiah. One last passage on this from the book of Revelation, Jesus himself declares:

*"I Jesus have sent mine angel to testify unto you these things in the churches. **I am the root and the offspring of David**, and the bright and morning star. And the Spirit and the bride say, Come. And let him that heareth say, Come. **And let him that is athirst come. And whosoever will, let him take the water of life freely.**"*
Revelation 22:16, 17, KJV

This verse makes it unmistakable that Jesus Christ, Yeshua the Messiah is the messianic ensign for Israel and the nations predicted by Isaiah the prophet. He is both the root-source (in His Divinity) and offspring-descendent (in His humanity) of David, whose father was Jesse, and the Savior that offers all to drink the water of life from the wells of salvation! Are you beginning to understand, God makes covenants and promises, and by keeping these, in ways more precise than we can imagine, He makes known to us that He truly is GOD.

In the *"fullness of time"* (Galatians 4:4) God instituted the New Covenant that he had promised to Israel. Yahweh establishes this covenant with whoever will believe and enter into it from Israel and the nations (Jeremiah 31:31-34, Matthew 26:26-28). We enter into this New Covenant with the Creator of the universe, who always keeps his promises, when we put our faith and hope in Jesus the *Messiah* for the forgiveness of sins! This is very good news! In case you were wondering, *Messiah* is a Hebrew word meaning "anointed one", *Christ* is derived from the Greek word meaning the same thing, and both are used in the New Testament to refer to the title and position of Jesus as promised King and Deliverer.

Satan, "god" of the fallen world system, is always looking to thwart God's purposes and attack his covenant people, the descendants of Israel and also, for the last 2 thousand years, the true believers in Jesus that make up the Church, the Body of Christ. The devil also works tirelessly to keep people from believing the message of salvation.

"But if our gospel be hid, it is hid to them that are lost: In whom the **god of this world** *hath blinded the minds of them which believe not, lest the light of the glorious gospel of Christ,*

who is the image of God, should shine unto them. For we preach not ourselves, but Christ Jesus the Lord; and ourselves your servants for Jesus' sake. For God, who commanded the light to shine out of darkness, hath shined in our hearts, to give the light of the knowledge of the glory of God in the face of Jesus Christ."
2 Corinthians 4:3-6, KJV

While the weakness of humanity because of sin and the seduction of Satan constantly drew Israel away from God, the work of Jesus on the cross finally provided what was needed to set people free from sin and the power of Satan for good. So while the enemy still exercises power over the nations as the "*god of this world*" (while unwittingly working out God's divine plan), **people who submit to God's authority through the gospel are set free from sins power and condemnation, and regain their lost authority on the earth in Christ, or rather, Christ's authority and power works through believers by faith.** (Proverbs 29:2, Luke 9:1, John 1:12, Mark 16, Luke 10:19, Acts 1:8).

Principle Seven: Understand God's Kingdom

Jesus the Messiah came to establish the Kingdom of God in the hearts of humanity by exposing and defeating the kingdom of darkness. In the Gospel of Mark, after his baptism by John, Jesus begins his ministry by proclaiming:

"The time is fulfilled, and the kingdom of God is at hand: repent ye, and believe the gospel." Mark 1:15, KJV

Mark's text then follows directly with the evidence that the Kingdom of God was taking root, by the fact that Jesus shows His authority over the kingdom of darkness.

"And there was in their synagogue a man with an unclean spirit; and he cried out, Saying, Let us alone; what have we to do with thee, thou Jesus of Nazareth? art thou come to destroy us? I know thee who thou art, the Holy One of God. And Jesus rebuked him, saying, Hold thy peace, and come out of him. And when the unclean spirit had torn him, and cried with a loud voice, he came out of him. And they were all amazed, insomuch that they questioned among themselves, saying, What thing is this? what new doctrine is this? for with authority commandeth he even the unclean spirits, and they do obey him."
Mark 1:23-27, KJV

What takes place when we accept Christ Jesus as Lord and Savior by turning from our sins against God (repenting), and rejecting any alliance with the kingdom of darkness, is declare our allegiance to the Kingdom of Heaven with Christ as our King. Until Christ returns in glory to judge the living and the dead, God's kingdom is established in the hearts of those who come to him, and work His will on the earth through the Holy Spirit.

"The law and the prophets were until John: since that time the kingdom of God is preached, and every man presseth into it."
Luke 16:16 KJV

"Now when He was asked by the Pharisees when the kingdom of God would come, He answered them and said, "The kingdom of God does not come with observation; "nor will they say, 'See here!' or 'See there!' For indeed, the kingdom of God is within you.""
Luke 17:20, 21, NKJV

Until Christ's return, God's kingdom is revealed through the lives of those who surrender to His Lordship. He rules in the hearts of those who surrender to Him, and then they manifest this new life to those around them. **It is important to know that living out the new life given in Christ is a process, so while the new birth promised is real and instant, growing and nurturing the new life in Christ is a process that all those**

who come to Him must walk out over time. In other words, **nobody is perfect, even those who have accepted the sacrifice of Christ on the cross**, but what they have done is place their feet on the path of fellowship with the love of God. We grow in relationship with God and with other believers into the image and glory of Christ through the indwelling presence of the Holy Spirit.

Principle Eight: Understand Why Christ Came – Part 1

To understand how to be set free, we must first understand why Jesus came:

1) Because of God's great love for us, to redeem mankind from the power of sin and its eternal consequences
2) To manifest God's kingdom and destroy the works of the Devil

Jesus came to redeem mankind from the power of sin and its eternal consequences:

*"And she shall bring forth a son, and thou shalt **call his name JESUS: for he shall save his people from their sins**."*
Matthew 1:21, KJV

All mankind is guilty of sin (unfaithfulness to Yahweh our Creator and transgression of His law), but God's free gift is justification (put back in good standing, just as if we never sinned) by grace through faith. This is the gospel, and the apostle Paul communicates it succinctly in his letter to the Romans:

"Obviously, the law applies to those to whom it was given, for its purpose is to keep people from having excuses and to bring the entire world into judgment before God. For no one can ever be made right in God's sight by doing what his law commands. For the more we know God's law, the clearer it becomes that we aren't obeying it.

But now God has shown us a different way of being right in his sight--not by obeying the law but by the way promised in the Scriptures long ago. **We are made right in God's sight when we trust in Jesus Christ to take away our sins***. And we all can be saved in this same way, no matter who we are or what we have done. For* **all have sinned; all fall short of God's glorious standard.** *Yet now God in his gracious* *kindness declares us not guilty. He has done this through Christ Jesus, who has freed us by taking away our sins. For* **God sent Jesus to take the punishment for our sins and to satisfy God's anger against us.**

We are made right with God when we believe that Jesus shed his blood, sacrificing his life for us. God was being entirely fair and just when he did not punish those who sinned in former times. And he is entirely fair and just in this present time when **he declares sinners to be right in his sight because they believe in Jesus."**
Romans 3:19-26, NLT

By saying "*for all have sinned*", the apostle is making sure everybody realizes we all are in the same sorry state, Jews and non-Jews, men, women and children, free or slave, pagan, atheist, monotheist, Catholic, Protestant, Muslim, Hindu, Buddhist, new ager etc. **We are all sinners, and sinners by nature have earned death. In addition, keeping the law cannot save us, because we are already lawbreakers.**

Yahweh outlined 10 over-arching principles to the people of Israel when he delivered them from the land of Egypt (Exodus 20:1-17). Known as the 10 Commandments (ten "*words*" or "*things*" in Hebrew), they can be briefly summarized as:

1) Yahweh alone is God, worship only Him
2) Do not make images of anything for the purpose of worshiping them (bowing down to them)
3) Do not take Yahweh's name in vain, do not blaspheme God our maker
4) Keep the Sabbath, the rest honors God and is good for people and their beasts of burden
5) Honor your Father and Mother
6) Do not commit murder
7) Do not commit adultery
8) Do not steal
9) Do not bear false witness (lie to get someone else in trouble)
10) Do not covet (desire to take or possess) anything that belongs to someone else

God expanded upon the 10 principles with specific worship rituals, holy days, festivals, and civic and moral statutes for the people of Israel. An explicit highlight of the worship rituals was the shedding of blood for forgiveness of sins in order to foreshadow the ultimate sacrifice of Jesus the Messiah on the cross. (Hebrews 10:1-14, see footnote for completed quote)[7]

God also summarized responsibility toward God and our fellow humanity more concisely in the two "greatest commandments": to **love Yahweh with all your heart, soul, mind, and strength** covering commands 1-4 (Deuteronomy 6:5, Matthew 22:37, Mark 12:30, Luke 10:27). And to **love your neighbor as yourself** which covers commands 5-10 (Leviticus 19:18, Matthew 22:39, Mark 12:31, Luke 10:27).

An honest self-assessment by anyone who has just read the 10 Commandments and the 2 Great Commandments listed above can only lead one to agree with the apostle's conclusion, we all have sinned. We have broken God's commandments!

The natural consequence of sin is death, both physical and spiritual:

"And the LORD God commanded the man, saying, "Of every tree of the garden you

*may freely eat; **"but of the tree of the knowledge of good and evil you shall not eat, for in the day that you eat of it you shall surely die."""***
Genesis 2:16, 17, NKJV

As previously discussed, Adam and Eve willfully transgressed the command of God under the Serpent's (Satan's) deceitful influence, rejecting God's kingdom and surrendering their dominion to Satan and entering into death, and all humanity has followed the pattern since then.

Satan's lie, "we will not die":

"Now the serpent was more cunning than any beast of the field which the LORD God had made. And he said to the woman, "Has God indeed said, 'You shall not eat of every tree of the garden'?" And the woman said to the serpent, "We may eat the fruit of the trees of the garden; "but of the fruit of the tree which is in the midst of the garden, God has said, 'You shall not eat it, nor shall you touch it, lest you die.'" ***Then the serpent said to the woman, "You will not surely die.*** *"For God knows that in the*

day you eat of it your eyes will be opened, and you will be like God, knowing good and evil." ***So when the woman saw that the tree was good for food, that it was pleasant to the eyes, and a tree desirable to make one wise, she took of its fruit and ate. She also gave to her husband with her, and he ate."***
Genesis 3:1-6, NKJV

Satan is still spreading the same lie, that sin will have no consequence, and we can be like "God", but thankfully God's Spirit through God's word exposes his lies. Sin brought death; instant spiritual death, progressive death of his soul and moral character, and after a gradual degradation of the body, finally physical death. This death was passed on to all the descendants of Adam and Eve:

"Wherefore, as by one man sin entered into the world, and death by sin; and so death passed upon all men, for that all have sinned [we already made this clear]*:"*
Romans 5:12, KJV

But God sent His Son to redeem and give eternal life!!! THIS IS THE GOOD NEWS!!!:

"For as in Adam all die, even so in Christ shall all be made alive."
1 Corinthians 15:22, KJV

"For the wages of sin is death; but the gift of God is eternal life through Jesus Christ our Lord."
Romans 6:23, KJV

Condemnation is not the message of Christ or the Bible, but rather comes from our sin of unbelief when we fail to put our trust in Jesus for salvation. It also comes from the *accuser*, another name for Satan (Revelation 12:10), who not only tempts us through our lusts, but also is right there to rub it in our faces when we fail.

"And I heard a loud voice saying in heaven, Now is come salvation, and strength, and the kingdom of our God, and the power of his Christ: ***for the accuser of our brethren is***

cast down, which accused them before our God day and night."
Revelation 12:10, KJV

Why would anyone refuse to come to Christ when we are already condemned by our own sins, and only Christ can set us free from this condemnation? Those who do come to Christ show their desire to be set free from sin by the drawing of the Holy Spirit, so they repent and accept the sacrifice of Christ on the cross. **The Holy Spirit is calling you to accept and believe this message:**

"For God so loved the world, that he gave his only begotten Son, that whosoever believeth in him should not perish, but have everlasting life. ***For God sent not his Son into the world to condemn the world; but that the world through him might be saved.*** *He that believeth on him is not condemned: but he that believeth not is condemned already, because he hath not believed in the name of the only begotten Son of God."*
John 3:16-18, KJV

"There is therefore now no condemnation to them which are in Christ Jesus, who walk not after the flesh, but after the Spirit."
Romans 8:1, KJV

All humanity is born into sin and is under the dominion of Satan, to enter God's kingdom requires "new birth" through the Holy Spirit of God. Even the most "religious" people need to come to Christ, because religion does not and cannot save, **only Jesus saves.** This includes all the religions of the world: Islam, Buddhism, Hinduism, animism, humanism, and even Christianity and Judaism. Sin is a killer, and without a substitute to take the penalty for our sins, every single individual is lost, as are the nations to which he or she belongs. Our only hope is to accept the free gift of God in the sacrifice of Jesus on the cross as atonement for our sins so that we can be born from above.

So, you might stop to ask, "Erik, are you saying that all I have to do to go to heaven is believe Jesus died for my sins and is risen from the dead?" And my answer would be "YES!"

"You mean my religion cannot save me?" And my answer would be "That is what I mean". Your religion cannot save you, even if it is "Christianity" if by "Christianity" you mean a system of rituals and observances. Every religious system in the world conditions the salvation of its adherents on fulfillment of certain tasks, "good works", religious observances, etc., and no one can ever be guaranteed that they have met the conditions.

The true faith presented in the Bible is that God has already met the conditions on our behalf in Jesus the Messiah, and we enter into HIS obedience by faith (the **gift** of righteousness), and allow HIM to take the consequences for our transgressions! The religious system God gave Moses foreshadowed this glorious truth, and now this foreshadowing is a reality! **Good works and thankfulness flow from a life already redeemed and guaranteed a seat at the heavenly table in Him!** Wouldn't you like to experience the peace and joy that comes from knowing your sins are forgiven, and eternal life is your inheritance through faith in Christ?

As proof that religion cannot save, even religious observance prescribed by God, Jesus declared that true salvation only comes through supernatural rebirth. This truth he shared with a religious leader on the ruling counsel of Israel.

"After dark one evening, a Jewish religious leader named Nicodemus, a Pharisee, came to speak with Jesus. "Teacher," he said, "we all know that God has sent you to teach us. Your miraculous signs are proof enough that God is with you." Jesus replied, "I assure you, unless you are born again, you can never see the Kingdom of God.""

Being very astute, Nicodemus replied:

""What do you mean?" exclaimed Nicodemus. "How can an old man go back into his mother's womb and be born again?"

Jesus replied, "The truth is, no one can enter the Kingdom of God without being born of water and the Spirit. Humans can reproduce only human life, but the Holy Spirit gives new life from heaven. So don't be surprised at my statement that you must be born again. Just as

you can hear the wind but can't tell where it comes from or where it is going, so you can't explain how people are born of the Spirit.""
John 3:1-3 and 4-8, NLT

"Therefore if any man be in Christ, he is a new creature: old things are passed away; behold, all things are become new." 2 Corinthians 5:17, KJV

You and I can enter into the new birth by answering the call of the Spirit to turn (repent) from our sins and human effort and put absolute faith in the finished work of Christ on the cross and his atoning blood, declaring that Jesus is LORD (Yahweh) and God, surrendering completely to His Lordship, yielding completely to His authority. Listen to what the apostle Peter said when asked by a crowed of people how to be saved:

"Then Peter said unto them, Repent, and be baptized every one of you in the name of Jesus Christ for the remission of sins, and ye shall receive the gift of the Holy Ghost."
Acts 2:38, KJV

In a similar way the apostle Paul said:

"For if you confess with your mouth that Jesus is Lord and believe in your heart that God raised him from the dead, you will be saved." Romans 10:9, NLT

Jesus Came to Set Free Those Who Have Suffered Because Of the Sins of Others

I have spent quite a bit of time reviewing the origin of sin, its consequences, and Christ's purpose in saving us from our sins. But we must spend a moment discussing how the sins of others affect us. **Sin brings death and damage to all it comes in contact with**. The presence of sin in the hearts of humanity quickly led to the murder of Abel by his brother Cain (Genesis 4:1-15). What is particularly grievous to the victims is that sometimes the deepest wounds are caused by the sins of those closest to us, even our own family members...husbands, wives, sisters, brothers, aunts, uncles, mothers and fathers. Teachers, coaches, politicians, or complete strangers can all be sources of sins against us. Sin in the hearts of humanity leads people to rob, mug, murder, rape, and kill. Sin leaves scars in the hearts of those who have been victims of the sins of others. The good news is that **Jesus also sets free and brings healing from the damage that the sins of others have caused us**.

The prophet Isaiah predicted the work that Jesus would do on the cross nearly 800 years before Christ was born, and Jesus perfectly fulfilled the prediction of Isaiah. The Holy Spirit revealed through Isaiah that Jesus the Messiah "*bore our griefs and carried our sorrows*", meaning he shares our burdens in this fallen world. The grief and sorrows that we are subjected to through no fault of our own, he has come to "break the yoke" of. The "*yoke*" is a symbol of servitude and bondage, being the harness used for beasts of burden to pull a plow. The breaking of the "*yoke*" symbolizes being set free. (Isaiah 10:27, 58:6, Jeremiah 30:8, Matthew 11:30, Galatian 5:1) The Hebrew word translated "*grief*" can also mean "*sickness*", and the word translated "*sorrow*" also means "*pain*". Deep heart wounds and psychological pain can be caused by the sins of others, and **even physical sickness can be the result of broken**

emotions and spiritual misdirection. Jesus *"was wounded for our transgressions, bruised for our iniquities"*; he paid the penalty for the sins we have personally committed. Christ suffered chastisement so that we could have peace, *"the chastisement of our peace was upon him"*. Open your heart to the words of the prophet Isaiah concerning Christ:

"Who has believed our message? To whom will the LORD reveal his saving power? My servant grew up in the LORD's presence like a tender green shoot, sprouting from a root in dry and sterile ground. There was nothing beautiful or majestic about his appearance, nothing to attract us to him. ***He was despised and rejected--a man of sorrows, acquainted with bitterest grief.*** *We turned our backs on him and looked the other way when he went by. He was despised, and we did not care.*

Yet ***it was our weaknesses he carried; it was our sorrows that weighed him down.*** *And we thought his troubles were a punishment from God for his own sins! But* ***he was wounded and crushed for our sins. He was beaten that we might have peace. He was whipped, and we were healed!***

All of us have strayed away like sheep. We have left God's paths to follow our own. Yet the LORD laid on him the guilt and sins of us all. *He was oppressed and treated harshly, yet he never said a word. He was led as a lamb to the slaughter. And as a sheep is silent before the shearers, he did not open his mouth. From prison and trial they led him away to his death. But* ***who among the people realized that he was dying for their sins--that he was suffering their punishment?*** *He had done no wrong, and he never deceived anyone. But he was buried like a criminal; he was put in a rich man's grave. But it was the LORD's good plan to crush him and fill him with grief.*

Yet when his life is made an offering for sin, he will have a multitude of children, many heirs. He will enjoy a long life, and the LORD's plan will prosper in his hands. When he sees all that is accomplished by his anguish, he will be satisfied. And ***because of what he has experienced, my righteous servant will make it possible for many to be counted righteous, for he will bear all their sins.*** *I will give him the honors of one who is mighty and great, because he exposed himself to death. He was counted among those who were sinners.* ***He***

bore the sins of many and interceded for sinners.*" Isaiah 53:1-12, NLT*

Dear reader, there is a whip mark, thorn piercing, wound on the hand, feet or side of Jesus Christ for every pain and wound caused to us by the sins of others, and a wound on Christ for every sin and wound we have caused. In other words, **complete and total redemption, salvation, and healing from sin can be found in Jesus Christ alone**. He is risen from the dead, and ever lives to make intercession, He is our advocate in heaven, for those who come to him by faith (Hebrews 7:25). That Christ would be the once for all sacrifice for sin was part of God's eternal plan, for he is the "*lamb slain from the foundation of the world*". (Hebrews 10:12, Revelation 13:8)

Fully entering into the healing available in Christ can take time to work through, and this book is really like a rocket launching pad to get you going in the right direction. We start by repenting from our own sins and forgiving those who have sinned against us.

After you have completed setting your feet on the path of salvation and deliverance in Christ discussed in this book, continued growth, healing, and closeness to God is nurtured by prayer (two way communication with Yahweh), scripture study, fellowship with other believers, and, if the wounds in your heart and soul are deep, or if torment continues, biblically sound, Christ centered counseling and ministry from someone who understands their authority in Jesus Christ over the kingdom of darkness.

Principle Eight: Understand why Christ Came – Part 2

"For this purpose the Son of God was manifested, that he might destroy the works of the devil."
1John 3:8b, KJV

Jesus Demonstrated Who He Was By His Authority Over Evil Spirits

Jesus demonstrates God's Kingdom through His authority over the kingdom of darkness. Lets take a moment to get a second look at the first miracle recorded in the gospel of Mark:

"Later on, after John was arrested by Herod Antipas, Jesus went to Galilee to preach God's Good News. "At last the time has come!" he announced. **"The Kingdom of God is near! Turn from your sins and believe this Good News!"** *... Jesus and his companions went to the town of Capernaum, and every Sabbath day he went into the synagogue and taught the people.* **They were amazed at his teaching, for he taught as one who had real authority**--*quite unlike the teachers of religious law. A man possessed by an evil spirit was in the synagogue, and he began shouting, "Why are you bothering us, Jesus of Nazareth? Have you come to destroy us? I know who you are--the Holy One sent from God!" Jesus cut him short. "Be silent! Come out of the man." At that, the evil spirit screamed and threw the man into a convulsion, but then he left him. Amazement gripped the audience, and they began to discuss what had happened.* **"What sort of new teaching is this?" they asked excitedly. "It has such authority! Even evil spirits obey his orders!""**
Mark 1:14-15, 21-27, NLT

Jesus the Messiah has all authority in heaven and on earth (Matthew 28:18). When you turn to him and accept his sacrifice on the cross, and believe in his resurrection from the dead, you are placing yourself in a position where **HIS** authority can come to bear in your life and you can be set free by **HIS** power. The apostle Paul prayed a powerful prayer for those who put their faith in Jesus Christ:

"Ever since I first heard of your strong faith in the Lord Jesus and your love for Christians everywhere, I have never stopped thanking God for you. I pray for you constantly, ***asking God, the glorious Father of our Lord Jesus Christ, to give you spiritual wisdom and understanding, so that you might grow in your knowledge of God.*** *I pray that your hearts will be flooded with light so that you can understand the wonderful future he has promised to those he called. I want you to realize what a rich and glorious inheritance he has given to his people.* ***I pray that you will begin to understand the incredible greatness of his power for us who believe him. This is the same mighty power that raised Christ from the dead and seated him in the place of honor at God's right hand in the heavenly realms. Now he is far above any***

ruler or authority or power or leader or anything else in this world or in the world to come. And God has put all things under the authority of Christ, *and he gave him this authority for the benefit of the church. And the church is his body; it is filled by Christ, who fills everything everywhere with his presence."*
Ephesians 1:15-23, NLT

Then the apostle goes on to explain what happens to those who put their faith in Christ:

*"And you He made alive, who were dead in trespasses and sins, in which you once walked according to the course of this world, according to the prince of the power of the air, the spirit who now works in the sons of disobedience, among whom also we all once conducted ourselves in the lusts of our flesh, fulfilling the desires of the flesh and of the mind, and were by nature children of wrath, just as the others. But **God, who is rich in mercy, because of His great love with which He loved us, even when we were dead in trespasses, made us alive together with Christ (by grace you have been saved), and raised us up together, and***

made us sit together in the heavenly places in Christ Jesus*, that in the ages to come He might show the exceeding riches of His grace in His kindness toward us in Christ Jesus. For **by grace you have been saved through faith, and that not of yourselves; it is the gift of God, not of works, lest anyone should boas**t. For we are His workmanship, created in Christ Jesus for good works, which God prepared beforehand that we should walk in them."*
Ephesians 2:1-10, NKJV

My question is; what else does it take to convince us of God's love for us? Even while we were completely "dead in sin", Jesus died on our behalf, will endow us with new life by faith in his work on the cross, and raises us up to sit with Him in heavenly places, this is where God's thrown is! This is why Satan is defeated, and why he is "hell bent", pun intended, in keeping you and I away from the truth that is found in the cross of Jesus Christ. **The devil uses all means at his disposal to keep people blinded to the truth.** Past hurts, deceptive religion, our own shame mixed with his condemnation in what we have done, what others have done to us... these are all tools used to keep us from faith in the glorious gospel. **All the while God is holding out the olive branch of peace to us through the sacrificial blood of the cross of Christ.**

Principle Nine: Occult Activity Opens Doors To Demonic Activity

Sin has not changed since the time of Adam and Eve, it still brings death, and still opens doors to entrapment by forces of darkness. While not always the case, habitual sin that cannot be stopped after someone comes to Christ might indicate demonic activity that needs to be broken. The same process by which humanity fell is reversed in our redemption. As was stated earlier, Adam's sin brought death, instant spiritual death, progressive death of the human soul and moral character, and a gradual degradation of the body, finally resulting in physical death.

Redemption follows the same pattern, we are first reborn, or "born of the Spirit", where God through the grace that is in Christ Jesus breaths new life into our innermost being, our "spirit" through the Holy Spirit (Romans 8:16). Then gradually over time our mind, will, and emotions are renewed by the Holy Spirit through the teaching of the word of God - the Holy Scriptures which is our spiritual nourishment, fellowship (loving communication and relationship) with God through prayer, and continued fellowship with other believers. Finally, our bodies are fully redeemed in the resurrection or, if we are alive at Christ's glorious return, the *rapture* - at the time of the resurrection of the dead in Christ, believers in Jesus Christ living at that time also partake of the resurrection without passing into death (1 Corinthians 15:51-52, 1 Thessalonians 4:13-18).

There is also physical healing, which God can choose to grace us with during our earthly pilgrimage before the final state of glory in the resurrection. Jesus displayed this during his earthly ministry, and the Holy Spirit has shown works of healing throughout the period of the new covenant church. In addition, certain physical symptoms can also be the result of demonic oppression, however, once the spirits are shown the exit door by the authority of Christ's name, these symptoms disappear. **Unbelievers and sometimes even Christians open doors of darkness by giving place to sins of the flesh (cheered on by evil forces of course), but especially by participating in occult activity and false religion.**

The word "occult" means "hidden" or "secret". The whole idea is that through the occult we are getting information "hidden" or unavailable through God's sanctioned means. Satan's temptation was, and still is, that there is "knowledge" available if one disobeys God's commands. The sources of this "hidden" knowledge are supernatural beings (or today they might claim to be space aliens), but God has made every effort to let us know this water comes from poison wells. There is just enough truth in the enemies' lie to hook the hearer, just like poison water may wet the pallet but kills in the long run. As seen in previous verses, because communication and cooperation with Satin led to deception and ultimately to the downfall of the human race (both before the Flood, Genesis chapters 3 and

6, and many nations after the flood, Genesis 10 and forward), attempts to communicate with the fallen spiritual realm were forbidden in the law God gave to Moses. Permitted forms of supernatural communication are:

1) Direct two-way communication with the Triune Creator God through the Holy Spirit, Scripture, and prayer. Why would anybody want to go through a "creature" rather than go straight to the Creator? He invites people to come directly to Him because He loves them.
2) God initiated communication by speaking through His gifts by the Holy Spirit given to His people, in agreement with the Scriptures. (1 Corinthians 12-14)
3) Rare communication from God's loyal holy angels – in line with clarification to follow.

God's angels always acknowledge their allegiance to Christ as LORD [Yahweh the Son], who became man to die for our sins. God's angels worship Jesus (Psalms 103:20; 148:2; Luke 2:13; Revelation 7:11), and **are not to be worshiped** (Revelation 22:8,9). If the spiritual messenger is not a worshiper of Jesus the Messiah, or fails to acknowledge the supremacy of Christ come in the flesh, you can be sure he is one of Satan's henchmen, angelic or human. In contrast to the devoted holy angels, evil spirits and fallen angels are more than willing to communicate with people in order to lead them away from Christ and the truth. Jesus said of those who resist **HIS** authority:

"Ye are of your father the devil, and the lusts of your father ye will do. He was a murderer from the beginning, and abode not in the truth, because there is no truth in him. When he speaketh a lie, he speaketh of his own: for he is a liar, and the father of it."
John 8:44, KJV

One person who I assisted in ministering Christ's deliverance (lets call this person "Sue" to protect her privacy) had opened doors by practicing the "Ouija" board, a "game" which is in reality an occult device used to communicate with evil spirits, as are Tarot cards, séances, crystal balls, and the like. Sue, who usually used the board with a friend, was using it alone one day when all of a sudden she heard a voice saying, "You are stubborn enough to possess"! She was discovered by her live-in boyfriend sitting in the middle of a room in the dead of a Michigan winter with all the windows open! I was asked to assist by an in-law of Sue when she began to exhibit these strange symptoms. They were thinking of having her committed.

Requesting they wait, I asked a sister in Christ named Debra from the church where I was youth minister to join me in visiting the victim of the demonic attack, an attack made possible by opening the door of the occult. I shared with Sue some of the same scriptures I am sharing in this book, and she prayed with us to give her heart to Christ. After Sue surrendered her life to Jesus, we addressed the demonic entities that were given admittance with the authority of Jesus Christ and command them to leave! Sue was completely set free from the forces that had entered, and the change in her face was clearly visible; A change from fear and oppression to one of relief, peace, and freedom.

You will be given an opportunity at the end of this book to give your life to Christ and use the authority given in Jesus name to deal with the enemy. If you are struggling or believe you need help beyond the purview of this work, seek help from a local ministry. Those who may be equipped to help you deal with the forces of darkness will be Pentecostal, Charismatic, or strong bible based communities. Take this book with you and let them know you would like them to help walk you through the steps at the end of this book.

The apostles of Jesus warned against listening to angels or any one else coming with a message contrary to the truth:

"But though we, or an angel from heaven, preach any other gospel unto you than that which we have preached unto you, let him be accursed."
Galatians 1:8, KJV

"And who is the great liar? The one who says that Jesus is not the Christ. Such people are

antichrists, for they have denied the Father and the Son. Anyone who denies the Son doesn't have the Father either. But anyone who confesses the Son has the Father also."
1 John 2:22, 23, NLT

"and every spirit that does not confess that Jesus Christ has come in the flesh is not of God. And this is the spirit of the Antichrist, which you have heard was coming, and is now already in the world."
1 John 4:3, NKJV

"For many deceivers are entered into the world, who confess not that Jesus Christ is come in the flesh. This is a deceiver and an antichrist."
2 John 1:7, KJV

Principle One Revisited: God Loves Us In Spite Of Our Failings

Let me emphasize again that God loves YOU. We are not sharing these passages to condemn you, but to open your mind to the truth! **Again, GOD wants to set you free, but we first have to understand what we need to be set free from. There are many false religions, and a great many of them started with an angelic visitation!** If you are or have been an adherent of one of these religions then you know what I am saying is true. Just a few of the religions that have their origins with angelic teaching or visitations of being(s) from another dimension are Islam, Mormonism, elements of Hinduism, New Age spirituality, and many animistic and pagan religions. **The difference between these and the Judeo-**

Christian angelic messages is that in the Bible, God's angels are brief, to the point, and always direct attention to God the Father and the Lord Jesus, never to themselves.

Principle Nine Continued: If It Was Wrong Then, It Is Wrong Today

The passages to follow clearly reveal that God forbids occult activity of all forms, witchcraft, astrology, sorcery, communication with departed spirits or ghosts (necromancy), sacrifice to other gods, making of idols, bestiality, human sacrifice, and the aberrant sexual practices that often accompany idolatrous worship, etc. **The rise in militant homosexuality, out of wedlock relationships, abortion, and divorce rates in Western culture is directly parallel to the rise of eastern and pagan religions, and the abandonment of Biblical truth in our institutions.** Many occult practices take place today, sometimes in very similar ways, to what took place in pagan ritual thousands of years ago. Others, like burning children in the fire or leaving them to exposure, have parallels in today's society like voluntary abortion as a means of birth control, not to mention direct satanic sacrificial and sex ritual.

Paganism and idolatry are once again becoming ingrained in Western culture, and this is evidenced by abortion (Psalms 22:9, 139:13, Isaiah 44:2), bodily mutilation (excessive piercings and tattoos, Deuteronomy 14:1, Leviticus 19:28), extra-marital sexual practices including; fornication, adultery, homosexuality, pedophilia, bestiality (Leviticus 20, Galatians 5:19-21). Spiritism (Leviticus 19:31), secular humanism and atheism (Psalm 14:1), Eastern "spirituality" (Isaiah 46 and 47), Satanism (Luke 4:6-7), astrology (Isaiah 47:13), and scientism (1 Timothy 6:20); all these are signs of the downward spiral. The first commandment still stands, *"Thou shalt have now no other gods before me"* (Ex 20:3).

Evil spirits teach evil things. Early after the great flood, from the tower of Babel till today, the nations of the earth were willing followers of this evil teaching, so God began a special relationship with Abraham and his descendants, the people of Israel, to begin weaning humanity from the lunacy of trusting false gods, and through Israel, eventually the other nations. The nation of Israel was blessed when they obeyed and walked with God, but Israel also provided an example of the results of rebellion against God through false religion and the occult.

*""When you arrive in the land the LORD your God is giving you, be very careful not to imitate the detestable customs of the nations living there. For example, never sacrifice your son or daughter as a burnt offering. And do not let your people practice fortune-telling or sorcery, or allow them to interpret omens, or engage in witchcraft, or cast spells, or function as mediums or psychics, or call forth the spirits of the dead. **Anyone who does these things is an object of horror and disgust to the LORD**. It is because the other nations have done these things that the LORD your God will drive them out ahead of you. You must be blameless before the LORD your God. The people you are about to displace consult with sorcerers and fortune-tellers, but the LORD your God forbids you to do such things."*

Deuteronomy 18:9-14, NLT

Aberrant sexual practice is directly associated with spiritual corruption.

"You shall not permit a sorceress to live. Whoever lies with an animal shall surely be put to death."
Exodus 22:18, 19, NKJV

While not capitol offenses outside of the ancient Israelite theocracy, the severity of the transgressions delineated and the depth of depravity they represent should not be underestimated. Satan relishes the opportunity to lead someone into his trap.

"Satan, the god of this evil world, has blinded the minds of those who don't believe, *so they are unable to see the glorious light of the Good News that is shining upon them. They don't understand the message we preach about the glory of Christ, who is the exact likeness of God."*
2 Corinthians 4:4, NLT

"From the time the world was created, people have seen the earth and sky and all that God made. They can clearly see his invisible qualities--his eternal power and divine nature. So they have no excuse whatsoever for not knowing God. Yes, they knew God, but they wouldn't worship him as God or even give him thanks. And they began to think up foolish ideas of what God was like. The result was that their minds became dark and confused. Claiming to be wise, they became utter fools instead. And instead of worshiping the glorious, ever-living God, they worshiped idols made to look like mere people, or birds and animals and snakes. So God let them go ahead and do whatever shameful things their hearts desired. As a result, they did vile and degrading things with each other's bodies. Instead of believing what they knew was the truth about God, they deliberately chose to believe lies. So they worshiped the things God made but not the Creator himself, who is to be praised forever. Amen."
Romans 1:20-25, NLT

There was a period in the history of the nation of Israel when they were taken captive to a nation called Babylon (located in modern day Iraq) as a disciplinary measure for 70 years. While God's purpose was being worked out at this time, still the motives and structure of the Babylonian society was deeply corrupt and aligned with the kingdom of darkness, as it had been since it origins under Nimrod. (Genesis 10:8-9; 11:1-9, Micah 5:6) God spoke these words against the rulers of Babylon, both earthly and spiritual. As you read the next passage, consider where our own society is headed, and search your own heart:

"Well, those two things will come upon you in a moment: widowhood and the loss of your children. Yes, these calamities will come upon you, despite all your witchcraft and magic. "You felt secure in all your wickedness. 'No one sees me,' you said. ***Your 'wisdom' and 'knowledge' have caused you to turn away from me and claim, 'I am self-sufficient and not accountable to anyone!'*** *So disaster will overtake you suddenly, and you won't be able to charm it away. Calamity will fall upon you, and you won't be able to buy your way out. A catastrophe will arise so fast that you won't know what hit you.* ***"Call out the demon hordes you have worshiped all these years.***

Ask them to help you strike terror into the hearts of people once again. You have more than enough advisers, astrologers, and stargazers. Let them stand up and save you from what the future holds. But they are as useless as dried grass burning in a fire. They cannot even save themselves! *You will get no help from them at all. Their hearth is not a place to sit for warmth."*
Isaiah 47:9-14, NLT

God considers stubbornness and the rejecting of His word akin to idolatry and witchcraft. Remember what the demonic entity said to "Sue" playing with the Ouija board, "you are stubborn enough to possess". Listen to what God said to the first king of Israel, Saul, a man who thought it was acceptable to offer a sacrifice instead of obey what God had commanded him to do. In other words he thought, "My little present to God will make up for my disobedience". It doesn't work that way!

"For rebellion is as the sin of witchcraft, and stubbornness is as iniquity and idolatry. Because thou hast rejected the word of the

LORD, he hath also rejected thee from being king."
1 Samuel 15:23, KJV

The worst thing we can do is to reject the word of Yahweh. Another evil king of Judah brought this biting prophetic condemnation of his actions:

"And he caused his children to pass through the fire in the valley of the son of Hinnom: also he observed times, and used enchantments, and used witchcraft, and dealt with a familiar spirit, and with wizards: he wrought much evil in the sight of the LORD, to provoke him to anger."
2 Chronicles 33:6, KJV

Well, are you starting to get the point. **There really are two kingdoms**, **the kingdom of God and the kingdom of darkness,** and everybody is in allegiance to one or the other. Each individual, actively or passively in the kingdom of darkness, is given the opportunity to pursue the kingdom of God, and the true life of His salvation.

*"I call heaven and earth to record this day against you, that I have set before you life and death, blessing and cursing: **therefore choose life**, that both thou and thy seed may live:" Deuteronomy 30:19, KJV*

*"Even when Gentiles [non-Israelite nations], who do not have God's written law, instinctively follow what the law says, they show that in their hearts they know right from wrong. They demonstrate that God's law is written within them, for their own consciences either accuse them or tell them they are doing what is right. **The day will surely come when God, by Jesus Christ, will judge everyone's secret life.** This is my message."*
Romans 2:14-16, NLT

Every human being is given a spark of righteousness in his or her conscience that can be fanned into a flame when faith is placed in the gospel.

The apostle of Christ lists some of the sins that Jesus came to set people free from. **He forgives, He heals, and He sets free if we will only turn from our sins to Him.**

*"When you follow the desires of your sinful nature, your lives will produce these evil results: sexual immorality, impure thoughts, eagerness for lustful pleasure, idolatry, participation in demonic activities, hostility, quarreling, jealousy, outbursts of anger, selfish ambition, divisions, the feeling that everyone is wrong except those in your own little group, envy, drunkenness, wild parties, and other kinds of sin. Let me tell you again, as I have before, that anyone living that sort of life will not inherit the Kingdom of God. **But when the Holy Spirit controls our lives, he will produce this kind of fruit in us: love, joy, peace, patience, kindness, goodness, faithfulness, gentleness, and self-control**. Here there is no conflict with the law."*
Galatians 5:19-23, NLT

To make it absolutely clear that we don't have to remain where we are, in 1 Corinthians 6:9-11, the apostle Paul gives a very similar list, and concludes it with:

"And such were some of you: but ye are washed, but ye are sanctified, but ye are

justified in the name of the Lord Jesus, and by the Spirit of our God."
1 Corinthians 6:11, KJV

The apostle also makes clear that false religion is not just a matter of a difference of opinion. **God is calling YOU to be set free from the power of the devil!**

"But I say, that the things which the Gentiles [citizens of non Israelite nations] *sacrifice, they sacrifice to devils [demons], and not to God: and I would not that ye should have fellowship with devils."*
1 Corinthians 10:20, KJV

All who come to Christ, truly turning from their sin and putting all their trust in Jesus' sacrifice for their sin, will share in God's kingdom. To reject Jesus is to remain in your sin. The apostle John writes in the book of Revelation, the last book of the Bible:

"Then I saw a new heaven and a new earth, for the old heaven and the old earth had disappeared. And the sea was also gone. And I saw the holy city, the new Jerusalem, coming

down from God out of heaven like a beautiful bride prepared for her husband. I heard a loud shout from the throne, saying, **"Look, the home of God is now among his people! He will live with them, and they will be his people. God himself will be with them. He will remove all of their sorrows, and there will be no more death or sorrow or crying or pain. For the old world and its evils are gone forever."** *And the one sitting on the throne said, "Look, I am making all things new!" And then he said to me, "Write this down, for what I tell you is trustworthy and true." And he also said, "It is finished! I am the Alpha and the Omega--the Beginning and the End.* **To all who are thirsty I will give the springs of the water of life without charge!** *All who are victorious will inherit all these blessings, and I will be their God, and they will be my children.* **But cowards who turn away from me, and unbelievers, and the corrupt, and murderers, and the immoral, and those who practice witchcraft, and idol worshipers, and all liars--their doom is in the lake that burns with fire and sulfur.** *This is the second death.""*
Revelation 21:1-8, NLT

The list of transgressors above is a list of those who have rejected the call to repentance and new birth. **They are not obligated to remain in their sin; they do so of their own accord.** Redemption has been offered and rejected. Allegiance with Satan results in sharing his condemnation, as Jesus said:

""But when the Son of Man comes in his glory, and all the angels with him, then he will sit upon his glorious throne. All the nations will be gathered in his presence, and he will separate them as a shepherd separates the sheep from the goats. He will place the sheep at his right hand and the goats at his left.

Then ***the King will say to those on the right, 'Come, you who are blessed by my Father, inherit the Kingdom prepared for you from the foundation of the world.***

...

"Then the King will turn to those on the left and say, 'Away with you, you cursed ones, into the eternal fire prepared for the Devil and his demons! *For I was hungry, and you didn't feed me. I was thirsty, and you didn't*

give me anything to drink. I was a stranger, and you didn't invite me into your home. I was naked, and you gave me no clothing. I was sick and in prison, and you didn't visit me.' "Then they will reply, 'Lord, when did we ever see you hungry or thirsty or a stranger or naked or sick or in prison, and not help you?' And he will answer, 'I assure you, when you refused to help the least of these my brothers and sisters, you were refusing to help me.' **And they will go away into eternal punishment, but the righteous will go into eternal life.""**
Matthew 25:31-46, NLT

Fallen angels and demons are deceptive, and can appear to be angels of light; we are not to believe any spirit, angelic or human, if it does not present the gospel of Christ – Jesus was born of a virgin, truly died on a cross as a sacrifice for sins, and was bodily raised from the dead the third day.

"I marvel that ye are so soon removed from him that called you into the grace of Christ unto another gospel: Which is not another; but there be some that trouble you, and would pervert the gospel of Christ. **But though we, or**

an angel from heaven, preach any other gospel unto you than that which we have preached unto you, let him be accursed. *As we said before, so say I now again, If any man preach any other gospel unto you than that ye have received, let him be accursed."*
Galatians 1:6-9, KJV

"For such are false apostles, deceitful workers, transforming themselves into the apostles of Christ. And no marvel; ***for Satan himself is transformed into an angel of light.****" 2 Corinthians 11:13, 14, KJV*

"Dear friends, do not believe everyone who claims to speak by the Spirit. You must test them to see if the spirit they have comes from God. For there are many false prophets in the world. This is the way to find out if they have the Spirit of God: If a prophet acknowledges that Jesus Christ became a human being, that person has the Spirit of God. If a prophet does not acknowledge Jesus, that person is not from God. Such a person has the spirit of the Antichrist. You have heard that he is going to come into the world, and he is already here."
1 John 4:1-3, NLT

Two observations:
1) Jesus Christ *"became a human being"*. That means that he:
    a. Pre-existed – *"God was manifest in the flesh"* (1 Timothy 3:16) so was truly Divine
    b. Was truly human – really became man. (John 1:14)
2) As an extension of becoming truly human, Jesus truly died on the cross (Philippians 2:8-11)

Anti-Semitism can also be a sign of demonic influence. Satan has always been against God's covenant people, and uses the anti-Semitism of the unregenerate to work his purposes, but God promises a blessing on those who bless Abraham and his covenant seed:

"Now the LORD had said to Abram: "Get out of your country, from your family and from your father's house, to a land that I will show you. I will make you a great nation; I will bless you and make your name great; and you shall be a blessing. ***I will bless those who bless you,***

and I will curse him who curses you; and in you all the families of the earth shall be blessed.""
Genesis 12:1-3, NKJV

Satan is always looking for ways to attack God's covenant people:

*"And the great dragon was cast out, that old serpent, called the Devil, and Satan, which deceiveth the whole world: he was cast out into the earth, and his angels were cast out with him. ... And when the dragon saw that he was cast unto the earth, **he persecuted the woman which brought forth the man child** [aka Israel]. ...And the dragon was wroth with the woman, **and went to make war with the remnant of her seed, which keep the commandments of God, and have the testimony of Jesus Christ** [true believers in Christ Jesus]." Revelation 12:9,13,17, KJV*

Deep-seated racism can also at times be demonic. This type of racism goes beyond cultural stereotypes and political incorrectness to an often hidden, irrational, deep-seated anger and/or hatred of certain ethnic group(s).

I say ethnic group because **the word "race" has been misconstrued by some to deny the common bond and origins of all humanity.** Satan hates people, all people, so creating animosity between them is one of his favorite tactics. Regardless of pigmentation and cultural differences, inspired Holy Scripture is clear that all people on this earth come from the common stock of Adam and Eve through Noah and his three sons.

*"And the sons of Noah, that went forth of the ark, were Shem, and Ham, and Japheth: and Ham is the father of Canaan. **These are the three sons of Noah: and of them was the whole earth overspread**."*
Genesis 9:18, 19, KJV

The apostle Paul makes it clear that ethnic distinctions are not a factor in acceptance into the Kingdom of God.

""God, who made the world and everything in it, since He is Lord of heaven and earth, does not dwell in temples made with hands. "Nor is He worshiped with men's hands, as though He needed anything, since He gives to

all life, breath, and all things. ***"And He has made from one blood every nation of men to dwell on all the face of the earth, and has determined their pre-appointed times and the boundaries of their dwellings, "so that they should seek the Lord, in the hope that they might grope for Him and find Him****, though He is not far from each one of us; "for in Him we live and move and have our being, as also some of your own poets have said, 'For we are also His offspring.'"*
Acts 17:24-28, NKJV

The human race, or the "children of Adam" as humanity is often referred to in the Bible, is really one race, with ethnic and cultural distinctions. As the transformative message of the gospel is received, God brings moral correctives to various elements of different cultures, but does not bring disdain on the unique contributions they make to a thriving humanity. We humans are all in the same situation as it relates to God; we are all sinners in need of a Savior.

"What then? are we better than they? No, in no wise: for we have before proved both

Jews and Gentiles [non-Jews, of the non-Israelite nations], *that they are all under sin; As it is written, There is none righteous, no, not one:" Romans 3:9, 10, KJV*

So, as there is no ethnic distinction (nor gender distinction for that matter) in our situation as it relates to God and our need for his salvation, there is also an equality of all within God's regenerated family, the family of those who have accepted the good news of Jesus's death, burial, and resurrection.

"For ye are all the children of God by faith in Christ Jesus. For as many of you as have been baptized into Christ have put on Christ. There is neither Jew nor Greek, there is neither bond nor free, there is neither male nor female: for ye are all one in Christ Jesus. *And if ye be Christ's, then are ye Abraham's seed, and heirs according to the promise."*
Galatians 3:26-29, KJV

Principle Ten: Only Sinners Can Be Set Free By Christ

Someone rightly once said, there is only one "kind" of person that can be saved by the work of Christ on the cross and enter God's kingdom, "the sinner kind". While the sins mentioned in the above passages are very serious, and the enemy is cunning and deceptive, Jesus came to set the captives free, and through him we can be set free! He offers **forgiveness**, **deliverance**, and **healing** as we call upon His name. In order to take advantage of the redemption that is in Christ, we have to come into agreement with God, which means acknowledging our sinfulness and need for His salvation. If we humble ourselves before God, he will raise us up. Pay careful attention to the things Jesus said:

*"The Spirit of the Lord is upon me, because he hath anointed me to preach the gospel to the poor; he hath sent me to **heal the brokenhearted**, to **preach deliverance to the captives**, and **recovering of sight to the blind**, to **set at liberty them that are bruised** [**wounded**], to **preach the acceptable year of the Lord**."*
Luke 4:18, 19, KJV

*"When evening had come, they brought to Him many who were demon-possessed. And He cast out the spirits with a word, and healed all who were sick, that it might be fulfilled which was spoken by Isaiah the prophet, saying: **"He Himself took our infirmities And bore our sicknesses.""***
Matthew 8:16, 17, NKJV

Jesus said:
"But if I with the finger of God cast out devils, no doubt the kingdom of God is come upon you."
Luke 11:20, KJV

Peter came to realize that the gospel of Jesus the Messiah [anointed one of God, Christ] was for the entire world, and for people of all nations after seeing a vision and being directed to go preach to a group of gentiles [member of a nation other than Israel]:

"Then Peter replied, ***"I see very clearly that God doesn't show partiality. In every nation he accepts those who fear him and do what is right. I'm sure you have heard about the Good News for the people of Israel--that there is peace with God through Jesus Christ, who is Lord of all.*** *You know what happened all through Judea, beginning in Galilee after John the Baptist began preaching. And no doubt you know that* ***God anointed Jesus of Nazareth with the Holy Spirit and with power. Then Jesus went around doing good and healing all who were oppressed by the Devil, for God was with him****. "And we apostles are witnesses of all he did throughout Israel and in Jerusalem.* ***They put him to death by crucifying him, but God raised him to life three days later.*** *Then God allowed him to appear, not to the general public, but to us whom God had chosen*

beforehand to be his witnesses. We were those who ate and drank with him after he rose from the dead. ***And he ordered us to preach everywhere and to testify that Jesus is ordained of God to be the judge of all--the living and the dead. He is the one all the prophets testified about, saying that everyone who believes in him will have their sins forgiven through his name.""***
Acts 10:34-43, NLT

The above passage makes it clear, that **Jesus, and Jesus alone will be the judge of the living and the dead. When we die we will appear before Jesus.** And Jesus will return and judge the nations. How joyful it will be to have placed your faith in his sacrifice and received forgiveness of sins before you stand before him to be judged for what you did in this earthly life!

Jesus shares his authority with those who put their trust in Him through the Holy Spirit, first to his disciples, and then to all who would believe the gospel:

"And the seventy returned again with joy, saying, Lord, even the devils are subject

unto us through thy name. And he said unto them, I beheld Satan as lightning fall from heaven. Behold, I give unto you power to tread on serpents and scorpions, and over all the power of the enemy: and nothing shall by any means hurt you. **Notwithstanding in this rejoice not, that the spirits are subject unto you; but rather rejoice, because your names are written in heaven.**"
Luke 10:17-20, KJV

The deliverance from evil spirits is a sure sign that the true gospel of Jesus Christ is being proclaimed and believed in, but we rejoice that our names are written in God's book of life in heaven. Often physical healing can be the result of deliverance from evil spirits:

"He that believeth and is baptized shall be saved; but he that believeth not shall be damned. And these signs shall follow them that believe; In my name shall they cast out devils [demons]...they will lay hands on the sick, and they will recover"
Mark 16:16-16, KJV

"Then Philip went down to the city of Samaria, and preached Christ unto them. **And the people with one accord gave heed unto those things which Philip spake, hearing and seeing the miracles which he did. For unclean spirits, crying with loud voice, came out of many that were possessed with them:** *and many taken with palsies, and that were lame, were healed. And* **there was great joy in that city."**
Acts 8:5-8, KJV.

NOW it is time for YOU to…

"Submit yourselves therefore to God. Resist the devil, and he will flee from you."
James 4:7, KJV

You now know all that you need to know to be forgiven and set free from all the power of the enemy by the love, grace, and power of God available in Jesus Christ the Savior.

How To Be Set Free

Now that you know from the authority of God's word, the Bible, these ten things:

1) God Loves You
2) The Big Mess - We are part of a fallen humanity, and are subservient to sin and Satan outside of Christ
3) Satan and his demons lie, deceive, and mean us harm
4) The consequence of sin is death and slavery to Satan
5) God's angels outnumber the fallen 2 to 1
6) God promised to set us free from sin and Satan's power
7) God's kingdom is established through the gospel of Jesus Christ

who is the KING of kings. His name, the name of JESUS, is above ALL names

8) Jesus came to set us free from bondage to sin and Satan
9) Occult activity opens doors to demonic activity and subjection to them
10) Only sinners can be set free by Christ – be humble before God

...It is time to put the truth to the test.

Repent – this means to turn away from your sin, and go in a completely different direction. You are turning your back to the kingdom of darkness and turning your face toward the kingdom of God in Jesus Christ.

Believe the Gospel – put your complete trust in the **atonement** of Christ on the cross - Jesus the righteous and innocent took the punishment we deserved. Act on what you believe. Call on the name of the Lord Jesus, and you will be saved! Then follow Him and seek His will for your life. The Bible is your guidebook. One brother, L.A. Marzulli, calls the

Bible the "guidebook to the supernatural", and by now you are beginning to understand why. Prayer is your means of intimacy and communication with your Savior and Lord.

The Bible makes clear God's promise that He will forgive you and set you free if you put your trust in him, ***it is time to act on what you have heard. It is time to give your life to Christ, and allow His truth to set you free.*** If you are willing to completely yield to Jesus Christ and make him your Lord (which means yield to Him as supreme authority in your life), then say the following two prayers, using them as guidelines for your own words or word for word with all your heart.

It will help to keep the following steps in mind, borrowed from a faithful servant of Christ, Bible teacher Derek Prince, from his video "Basics of Deliverance". (Taken from notes written in my Bible in 1988 while watching the video in Jerusalem)

Derek Prince's Steps to Deliverance

1) Be Humble
2) Be Honest – you must choose between dignity and deliverance
3) Confess faith in Jesus Christ (He is the High Priest of our Confession Hebrews 3:1)
4) Confess any known sin committed by yourself or ancestors
5) Repent of ALL sin – Repent and Forsake (Proverbs 28:13)
6) Break with the Occult, Curses, and Secret Societies. Renounce.
7) Forgive Others
8) EXPEL (let them leave, exhale, cough, etc.)

A Prayer To Receive Christ

(Use as a guideline for your own words, or say it word for word with all your heart)

"Dear Father in Heaven,

I confess that I have sinned against you, and this very moment repent of all my sin and turn to you for forgiveness. You said, "Anyone that comes to you, you will not turn away".

Save me Lord Jesus, come into my heart and make me a new person, wash away my sin by your blood, and I will be whiter than snow. I put all my faith and trust in you for my salvation, and I forsake all the works of the flesh and attempts on my own strength to save myself, only you can save, only you can heal, only you can deliver. So save me Lord Jesus, heal me Lord Jesus, and deliver me Lord Jesus.

Thank you for your everlasting love toward me. I believe you died on the cross, and arose from the tomb on the third day, and I believe you will raise me up to be with you for all eternity because I place my hope and trust in you. I surrender to you as my Lord and God. Fill me with your Holy Spirit, and set me free by your blood. Give me a hunger and thirst for your word and the things of righteousness...

Thank you Heavenly Father for sending Jesus, and thank you Jesus for saving me and setting me free, and thank you Holy Spirit for leading me to Christ, Amen!"

A Prayer For Deliverance From Evil Spirits

(Pray it with all your heart, with conviction and the authority of a child of the KING!)

"Dear God,

As your child, I renounce all the evil works of darkness. Right now I confess and forsake (name your sins) ...
I repent of all association with the occult, witchcraft, and evil powers...(name any), and I renounce all allegiance to Satan and the kingdom of darkness, and claim full allegiance to Your kingdom and rule in my life.
I forgive those who have sinned against me, in particular (name them)...

In the name of Jesus through the cleansing of His blood I break all curses spoken against me, and my participation in any curse (name any that come to mind)...

I repent of any anti-Semitism I may have held in my heart, and pronounce a blessing on the people of Israel, and pray for their salvation in Christ.

I repent from and renounce all racism.

In the name of Jesus, and by His grace and authority in the blood of Jesus the Lamb of God, I command all evil spirits to release their hold on my mind and body, and command them to leave and go in the name of Jesus!

Go evil spirits, all unclean spirits and spirits of infirmity I command you to go in the name of Jesus!

I repent of all unholy sexual practices,
All spirits of lust and perversion and addiction I command you to go in the name of Jesus.
(name any specific thing the Holy Spirit brings to your mind)

All spirits of anger, hatred, evil, and unforgiveness I command you to go in the name of Jesus.

In the name of Jesus I am free, and who the SON sets free, is free indeed! (Feel free to repeat this proclamation until it sinks into your soul and spirit)

Dear God, completely immerse me in your Holy Spirit, empower me for your glory, and to proclaim your kingdom...
HALLEHLUJAH Praise you Jesus, Praise God...! (Continue to praise God for his goodness and deliverance through the blood of Jesus)"

...Continue to pray from your heart the words God gives you, rejoice in the wonderful grace of God, and be completely set free! Praise and think God for his goodness.

Proclamation Of Deliverance

Proclamation is powerful way to give notice to the spiritual realm that you are serious about God's truth. The word *proclaim* as defined by the American Heritage Dictionary means "to announce officially and publicly; declare", "to indicate unmistakable; make plain", and "to praise; extol". When we proclaim God's truth, we are making it official, public, and plain that we mean to follow God and give Him praise.

The great king of Israel David wrote in one of his songs:

*"Sing to the LORD, all the earth; **Proclaim** the good news of His salvation from day to day."*
1 Chronicles 16:23 and Psalm 96:2, NKJV

And the apostle Peter writes:

*"But you are a chosen generation, a royal priesthood, a holy nation, His own special people, that you may **proclaim** the praises of Him who called you out of darkness into His marvelous light;" 1 Peter 2:9, NKJV*

Speak these scriptural proclamations out loud, shout them if necessary, and recite them whenever you are under temptation, depression, or attack of the enemy. Give God all the glory and credit for setting you free. The Bible passages where these proclamations come from follow in the next chapter.

- I believe Jesus is Lord and he arose from the dead, and I am saved!
- I am a new creation in Christ Jesus!
- By Jesus' stripes I am healed!
- Jesus Christ has set me free!
- Jesus has destroyed all the power of the devil!

- Jesus loves me!
- I am accepted in Christ the beloved!
- I am a child of God, born of the Spirit!
- I am the righteousness of God in Christ Jesus!
- I am set free from sin!
- I am dead to sin in Christ, and I am risen with Him and seated with Him in heavenly places, far above all principality and power and might and dominion and any name that is named!
- I have been translated from the kingdom of darkness into the kingdom of God's dear Son, and am under the reign of Jesus Christ, King of Kings and Lord of Lords!
- I have been given the Spirit of Love, Power and a SOUND MIND!
- I will worship God the Father, God the Son, and God the Holy Spirit, the Holy Three in One all the days of my life!
- No weapon formed against me shall prosper!
- I am not condemned, for there is now no condemnation for those who are in

Christ Jesus, for I will walk in the Spirit, and not in the flesh!
- My weapons are spiritual and mighty, by which I will wage a good fight, pull down strongholds, cast down imaginations and bring every thought into obedience of Christ!
- I put on the full armor of God:
  - The belt of truth, Jesus is the way, the truth and the life, and God's word is truth.
  - I put on the breastplate of righteousness; I am the righteousness of God in Christ Jesus.
  - I wear the shoes of the gospel of peace, I am at peace with God through the work of the cross, and I will share this good news with others.
  - I take up the shield of faith, trusting in God's word and promises to quench the lies of the enemy.
  - I put on the helmet of salvation, the knowledge that I am saved by Christ alone.
  - And I take up the sword of the Spirit, the word of God, and I

commit to learning it, and hiding it in my heart, so I can use it effectively.

Scriptural Passages For Memory And Meditation

Commit these verses to memory if possible; they support the proclamations you just made. I have used the King James Version (except for the armor of God passage), but use whatever translation you like best.

"That if thou shalt confess with thy mouth the Lord Jesus, and shalt believe in thine heart that God hath raised him from the dead, thou shalt be saved."
Romans 10:9, KJV

"Therefore if any man be in Christ, he is a new creature: old things are passed away; behold, all things are become new."
2 Corinthians 5:17, KJV

"But he was wounded for our transgressions, he was bruised for our iniquities: the chastisement of our peace was upon him; and with his stripes we are healed."
Isaiah 53:5, KJV

"If the Son therefore shall make you free, ye shall be free indeed."
John 8:36, KJV

"For this purpose the Son of God was manifested, that he might destroy the works of the devil."
1John 3:8b

OK, for this one, just pick the verse or verses that really speak to you, unless you are ambitious:

"Wherefore I also, after I heard of your faith in the Lord Jesus, and love unto all the saints, Cease not to give thanks for you, making mention of you in my prayers; That the God of

our Lord Jesus Christ, the Father of glory, may give unto you the spirit of wisdom and revelation in the knowledge of him: The eyes of your understanding being enlightened; that ye may know what is the hope of his calling, and what the riches of the glory of his inheritance in the saints, And what is the exceeding greatness of his power to us-ward who believe, according to the working of his mighty power, Which he wrought in Christ, when he raised him from the dead, and set him at his own right hand in the heavenly places, Far above all principality, and power, and might, and dominion, and every name that is named, not only in this world, but also in that which is to come: And hath put all things under his feet, and gave him to be the head over all things to the church, Which is his body, the fulness of him that filleth all in all.

And you hath he quickened [made alive], who were dead in trespasses and sins; Wherein in time past ye walked according to the course of this world, according to the prince of the power of the air, the spirit that now worketh in the children of disobedience: Among whom also we all had our conversation in times past in the lusts of our flesh, fulfilling the desires of the flesh and of the mind; and were by nature the

children of wrath, even as others. But God, who is rich in mercy, for his great love wherewith he loved us, Even when we were dead in sins, hath quickened [made alive] *us together with Christ, (by grace ye are saved;) And hath raised us up together, and made us sit together in heavenly places in Christ Jesus: That in the ages to come he might shew the exceeding riches of his grace in his kindness toward us through Christ Jesus. For by grace are ye saved through faith; and that not of yourselves: it is the gift of God: Not of works, lest any man should boast."*
Ephesians 1:15-2:9, KJV

"Blessed be the God and Father of our Lord Jesus Christ, who hath blessed us with all spiritual blessings in heavenly places in Christ: According as he hath chosen us in him before the foundation of the world, that we should be holy and without blame before him in love: Having predestinated us unto the adoption of children by Jesus Christ to himself, according to the good pleasure of his will, To the praise of the glory of his grace, wherein he hath made us accepted in the beloved."
Ephesians 1:3-6, KJV

"For he hath made him to be sin for us, who knew no sin; that we might be made the righteousness of God in him."
2 Corinthians 5:21, KJV

"For sin shall not have dominion over you: for ye are not under the law, but under grace.
...Being then made free from sin, ye became the servants of righteousness. ...But now being made free from sin, and become servants to God, ye have your fruit unto holiness, and the end everlasting life. For the wages of sin is death; but the gift of God is eternal life through Jesus Christ our Lord."
Romans 6:14,18,22-23 KJV

"Giving thanks unto the Father, which hath made us meet to be partakers of the inheritance of the saints in light: Who hath delivered us from the power of darkness, and hath translated us into the kingdom of his dear Son: In whom we have redemption through his blood, even the forgiveness of sins: Who is the image of the invisible God, the firstborn of every creature: For by him were all things created, that are in heaven, and that are in earth, visible

and invisible, whether they be thrones, or dominions, or principalities, or powers: all things were created by him, and for him: And he is before all things, and by him all things consist."
Colossians 1:12-17, KJV

"For God hath not given us the spirit of fear; but of power, and of love, and of a sound mind."
2 Timothy 1:7, KJV

"The grace of the Lord Jesus Christ, and the love of God [the Father], and the communion of the Holy Ghost, be with you all. Amen.
2 Corinthians 13:14, KJV

"No weapon that is formed against thee shall prosper; and every tongue that shall rise against thee in judgment thou shalt condemn. This is the heritage of the servants of the LORD, and their righteousness is of me, saith the LORD."
Isaiah 54:17, KJV

"There is therefore now no condemnation to them which are in Christ Jesus,

who walk not after the flesh, but after the Spirit."
Romans 8:1, KJV

"For though we walk in the flesh, we do not war after the flesh: (For the weapons of our warfare are not carnal, but mighty through God to the pulling down of strong holds;) Casting down imaginations, and every high thing that exalteth itself against the knowledge of God, and bringing into captivity every thought to the obedience of Christ;"
2 Corinthians 10:3-5, KJV

"This charge I commit unto thee, son Timothy, according to the prophecies which went before on thee, that thou by them mightest war a good warfare"
1 Timothy 1:18, KJV

"A final word: Be strong with the Lord's mighty power. Put on all of God's armor so that you will be able to stand firm against all strategies and tricks of the Devil. For we are not fighting against people made of flesh and blood, but against the evil rulers and authorities of the unseen world, against those mighty powers of

darkness who rule this world, and against wicked spirits in the heavenly realms. Use every piece of God's armor to resist the enemy in the time of evil, so that after the battle you will still be standing firm. Stand your ground, putting on the sturdy belt of truth and the body armor of God's righteousness. For shoes, put on the peace that comes from the Good News, so that you will be fully prepared. In every battle you will need faith as your shield to stop the fiery arrows aimed at you by Satan. Put on salvation as your helmet, and take the sword of the Spirit, which is the word of God. Pray at all times and on every occasion in the power of the Holy Spirit. Stay alert and be persistent in your prayers for all Christians everywhere."
Ephesians 6:10-18, NLT

Conclusion

My dear brother or sister, if you have read this and followed all the steps with a sincere heart putting your faith and trust in Christ, you are a child of God, the Creator of the universe! Know you are loved, and God is with you until the end. **Yahweh God is faithful, and He keeps His covenant promises**. You are set free from the forces of darkness and seated with Christ in heavenly places. Seek God in His word the Bible using whatever translation you prefer, because the Word of God is where you find the truth, and the truth is your weapon against the lies of Satan. God is only a prayer away, so spend time with Him in prayer every day.

If you haven't yet, ask Him to fill you and baptize you in His Holy Spirit, and seek other Bible believing Christians to fellowship with and be encouraged by. Share with someone the good things that God has done for you. Follow the Lord and be baptized in water.

Do not fall into condemnation; all true believers in Christ have gone through similar experiences. We are all sinners, but in Christ, the true "Vine" we are set apart as saints. No one is righteous in their own strength before God but we all have to come to the cross of Christ for cleansing from sin, so please do not be shy in asking other Christians to come along side with you and pray with you and help you in your struggles. Be humble and willing to face any temporal consequences in the love and grace of God, knowing you have an eternity with God in heaven to look forward to. You will find love and encouragement in Christ's true body, the Church (assembly) of the redeemed.

Below is a song (Psalm) of encouragement written by one of God's friends under the inspiration of the Holy Spirit, king David of Israel, three thousand years ago. These words are just as true today and are offered as encouragement to you as you enter into your new life to Christ. God is also offering to you the hand of friendship!

A Psalm of David

"Praise the LORD, I tell myself; with my whole heart, I will praise his holy name. Praise the LORD, I tell myself, and never forget the good things he does for me. He forgives all my sins and heals all my diseases. He ransoms me from death and surrounds me with love and tender mercies. He fills my life with good things. My youth is renewed like the eagle's!

The LORD gives righteousness and justice to all who are treated unfairly. He revealed his character to Moses and his deeds to the people of Israel.

The LORD is merciful and gracious; he is slow to get angry and full of unfailing love. He will not constantly accuse us, nor remain angry forever. He has not punished us for all our sins, nor does he deal with us as we deserve. For his unfailing love toward those who fear him is as great as the height of the heavens above the earth. He has removed our rebellious acts as far away from us as the east is from the west.

The LORD is like a father to his children, tender and compassionate to those who fear him. For he understands how weak we are; he knows we are only dust. Our days on earth are like grass; like wildflowers, we bloom and die. The wind blows, and we are gone--as though we had never been here. But the love of the LORD remains forever with those who fear him. His salvation extends to the children's children of those who are faithful to his covenant, of those who obey his commandments!

The LORD has made the heavens his throne; from there he rules over everything. Praise the LORD, you angels of his, you mighty creatures who carry out his plans, listening for each of his commands. Yes, praise the LORD, you armies of angels who serve him and do his will! Praise the LORD, everything he has created, everywhere in his kingdom. As for me--I, too, will praise the LORD."
Psalms 103 NLT

May God bless you and keep you and make His face to shine upon you, and grant you peace! So be it, amen!

Erik A. Windischman

For more information, visit:

www.thekingdomparadigm.com

For resources by Derek Prince:

http://www.derekprince.org

Remedial Glossary Of Biblical Terms **

**While not exhaustive, we hope the reader unfamiliar with Biblical concepts finds this information helpful. Liberty comes from knowing the truth, understanding the truth, believing the truth and acting on the truth.

"And ye shall know the truth, and the truth shall make you free."
John 8:32, KJV

God – English translation of the Old Testament Hebrew word *"elohim"* or the New Testament Greek word *"theos"*. The Hebrew term, while a plural form of *"el" or "eloa"*, when used with the singular pronoun refers to the supreme Deity, the creator of all that is. Of the 2630 times *"elohim"* occurs in the Hebrew, it refers to the Creator and is translated with capitol "G" "God" 2346 times in the King James Version.

*"In the beginning **God** [Elohim] created the heaven[s] and the earth."*
Genesis 1:1, KJV

In the singular, used with plural pronouns, or as general context dictates, it can refer to lesser spiritual beings like angels and will be translated with the little "g", "god".

*"God standeth in the congregation of the mighty; he judgeth among the **gods**."*
Psalms 82:1, KJV

In particular, little "g" gods can refer to fallen sinful beings seeking the worship of humanity through the images that represent them:

*"Take heed to yourselves, that your heart be not deceived, and ye turn aside, and serve other **gods**, and worship them;"*
Deuteronomy 11:16, KJV

"But I say, that the things which the Gentiles sacrifice, they sacrifice to devils [demons], and not to God ["Theos", Greek for the supreme Deity]: *and I would not that ye should have fellowship with devils* [demons]*."*
1 Corinthians 10:20, KJV

Or, humanity creating their own false deities out of their vain imagination, or as representations of the lesser beings:

*"Turn ye not unto idols, nor make to yourselves molten **gods**: I am the LORD [Yahweh] your God [Elohim]."*
Leviticus 19:4, KJV

So to summarize the Biblical teaching, a "god" is part of a class of beings outside of our material time/space dimension.[8] God with a capitol "G" is the Supreme Being who brings everything into existence, material and immaterial, including the little "g" gods. The little "g" gods are not really "gods" in the sense of being worthy of worship, but the wicked ones presumptuously take it to themselves, in keeping with the prince of usurpers himself, Satan. This "god" or so he wishes, even tried to get Jesus to worship him, because as humanity's representative, Jesus was tempted in all the ways that humans are, yet without giving in to sin.

"And the devil said unto him, All this power will I give thee, and the glory of them: for

that is delivered unto me; and to whomsoever I will I give it. If thou therefore wilt worship me, all shall be thine. And Jesus answered and said unto him, Get thee behind me, Satan: for it is written, Thou shalt worship the Lord thy God, and him only shalt thou serve."
Luke 4:6-8, KJV

Yahweh – The English *transliteration* - letters and sounds of one language transposed to another - of God's holy, personal, covenant name "יהוה". Commonly called the "*tetragrammaton*" by scholars, and "*ha Shem*" or "the name" by devote Jews, the proper name of our Creator is often translated as LORD, in all capitols, or when used with "*Adonai*", אדני – Hebrew for Lord, then it is translated as "GOD" in all capitol letters. "Jehovah" is another common transliteration. The Jewish scribes and Masoretes of the 6th – 10th century, in order to avoid taking God's name in vain during reading, used the vowel pointing or "*nikkudot*" of "*Adonai*", so when the Hebrew text is read, the reader pronounces "*Adonai*", and not the actual name of God. When the vowels from "*Adonai*" are pronounced with the letters of Gods name, something akin to "Jehovah" is the resulting pronunciation.

While God [*Elohim*] Creator of the Universe is *what* He is, Yahweh is *who* He is; Yahweh is His Name. He has revealed himself as such. When Moses asked God his name God replied as follows.

"And God said unto Moses, I AM THAT I AM: and he said, Thus shalt thou say unto the children of Israel, I AM hath sent me unto you." Exodus 3:14, KJV

God said His name is the indefinite Hebrew verb "to be". He spoke it in the first person referring to Himself, "I AM" or "I WILL BE". The 3rd person form of this verb is the aforementioned Hebrew word transliterated as "*Yahweh*" and is literally, "HE IS" or "HE WILL BE".

This has implications when contemplating Jesus' claims. The prophet Isaiah, speaking in the voice of Yahweh proclaimed:

"Come ye near unto me, hear ye this; I have not spoken in secret from the beginning;

*from the time that it was, there **am I**: and now **the Lord GOD** [Yahweh], and **his Spirit**, hath sent **me**. Thus saith the **LORD** [Yahweh], thy Redeemer, the Holy One of Israel; **I am** the **LORD** [Yahweh] thy God which teacheth thee to profit, which leadeth thee by the way that thou shouldest go."*
Isaiah 48:16, 17, KJV

An alternative translation of *"and now the Lord GOD, and his Spirit, hath sent me"* would be *"and now the Lord GOD has sent me and his Spirit"*.

While challenging to fully comprehend, the passage from Isaiah quoted above makes clear that Yahweh has revealed Himself as "Lord [*Adonai*] Yahweh", the "Spirit [*Ruach*]" of Yahweh, and "Yahweh the Redeemer, the Holy One of Israel". Yahweh is a triune being, who came to be understood further by the revelation in the New Testament as God the Father, God the Son (or Word), and God the Holy Spirit, the three in One and One in Three, the blessed Trinity ("Trinity" is an extra biblical term describing the biblical revelation).

The passage from Isaiah just quoted says that the "me" speaking is Yahweh the "Redeemer, the Holy One of Israel" While there are many, a few New Testament passages will suffice to establish Jesus or *"Yeshua"* as discussed under the "Salvation" entry is Yahweh.

Jesus is the "Holy One" of Israel. Only Yahweh is the Holy One of Israel:

Peter declared during his sermon at the temple:

*"But ye denied **the Holy One** and the Just, and desired a murderer to be granted unto you;"*
Acts 3:14 KJV

Jesus, as the Word become flesh, is the Creator. Only Yahweh is the Creator:

"In the beginning was the Word, and the Word was with God, and the Word was God. The same was in the beginning with God. All things were made by him; and without him was not any thing made that was made...And the Word

was made flesh, and dwelt among us, (and we beheld his glory, the glory as of the only begotten of the Father,) full of grace and truth."
John 1:1-3,14 KJV

Jesus is the great "I AM". Only Yahweh is the Great "I AM":

*"Your father Abraham rejoiced to see my day: and he saw it, and was glad. Then said the Jews unto him, Thou art not yet fifty years old, and hast thou seen Abraham? Jesus said unto them, Verily, verily, I say unto you, Before Abraham was, **I am**."*
John 8:56-58, KJV

To summarize, the Old Testament revealed Yahweh as One eternal being in three unique "persons" for lack of a better term, the Father, the Word (Son), and the Holy Spirit, and this was made clearer and more distinct when God the Word took upon himself human flesh to die for the sins of the world. God was present in the opening chapters of Genesis as the **Father God creating**, speaking **his Word** to create the light and all else, with **His Spirit** brooding to bring it to pass.

*"In the beginning **God created** the heaven and the earth. And the earth was without form, and void; and darkness was upon the face of the deep. And **the Spirit of God** moved upon the face of the waters. And **God said [proclaimed His WORD]**, Let there be light: and there was light." Genesis 1:1-3, KJV*

God is One Yahweh:

"Hear, O Israel: The LORD our God is one LORD:"
Deuteronomy 6:4, KJV

The Word of the LORD is understood to be a person, only a person can come to someone and speak:

*"After these things **the word of the LORD came unto Abram in a vision, saying**, Fear not, Abram: I am thy shield, and thy exceeding great reward."*
Genesis 15:1, KJV

The Word, our Savior, became flesh:

"And the Word was made [became] flesh, and dwelt among us, and we beheld his glory, the glory as of the only begotten of the Father, full of grace and truth."
John 1:14, KJV

Jesus, the Word become flesh, after making atonement for the whole world, sends the Holy Spirit (who is Yahweh) from the Father (who is Yahweh):

"But when the Comforter is come, whom I will send unto you from the Father, even the Spirit of truth, which proceedeth from the Father, he shall testify of me:"
John 15:26, KJV

Idol - An idol is an image created by man to represent a little "g" god to be used in worship of the same. This is and has always been a very bad idea! Humans are not supposed to worship other creatures, only our Creator God! Humanity has historically gone rampant in their worship of and being seduced by other "gods". Sexual perversity is very closely affiliated with departure from spiritual truth.

"Professing themselves to be wise, they became fools, And changed the glory of the uncorruptible God into an image made like to corruptible man, and to birds, and fourfooted beasts, and creeping things. **Wherefore God also gave them up to uncleanness through the lusts of their own hearts, to dishonour their own bodies between themselves:** *Who changed the truth of God into a lie, and worshipped and served the creature more than the Creator, who is blessed for ever. Amen."*
Romans 1:22-25, KJV

The footholds of the invasive beings need to be broken by the power of God's word, His Spirit, and the blood of Jesus. The idols that represent them need to be destroyed.

Another sense of "idol" is any thing in our lives that takes precedence over loving and serving God. Even things that under normal circumstances are fine and good can become idols. Food can become an idol, alcohol an idol, electronic games can be an idol; sex has become a major idol in our culture. Basically **any object or activity that we place higher**

in our chain of priorities than loving and serving God in Christ Jesus becomes an idol.

Salvation – The English word "salvation" means "preservation or deliverance from evil or difficulty". This word translates the Hebrew word *"yeshuah"*, and in fact Jesus' name in Hebrew, *"Yeshua"*, is the same word! The Greek word translated "salvation", with the same general meaning is *"soterion"*. The angel announced to Joseph that he needed to name the child born to his virgin wife "Yeshua", or Jesus (as transliterated from Hebrew to Greek to English) in English:

*"But while he thought on these things, behold, the angel of the Lord appeared unto him in a dream, saying, Joseph, thou son of David, fear not to take unto thee Mary thy wife: for that which is conceived in her is of the Holy Ghost. And she shall bring forth a son, and thou shalt call his name **JESUS** [Yeshua, Salvation]: **for he shall save his people from their sins."** Matthew 1:20, 21, KJV*

Salvation, or deliverance is illustrated in its most practical sense by the event of the Exodus of the Hebrew slaves from Egypt.

1) They were delivered from cruel slavery (Exodus 1:14; 3:8)
2) They were "passed over" during God's judgment on the pagan nation of Egypt (Exodus 12:13)
3) Their enemies and the gods they worshiped were judged (Exodus 12:12)
4) As long as they were obedient, the Hebrew slaves were led to a blessed life of dependence on and relationship with the LORD their God (Deuteronomy 28:1-14)
5) They were made a kingdom of priests and a witness to the nations (Exodus 19:3-6, Deuteronomy 4:6)

The salvation that God gives through Jesus is directly parallel with the salvation of Israel from Egypt:

1) The New Covenant believer is delivered from the slavery of sin (Matthew 1:21, Acts 22:16, 1 Titus 1:15)
2) The enduring New Covenant believer is completely forgiven of all sin, and will be "passed over" when God judges the nations (Romans 5:8-9; 1 Corinthians 5:7, 1 Thessalonians 5:9)
3) The "god of this world", Satan, has been judged (John 15:7-11, 1 John 3:8, Revelation 20:10)
4) The New Covenant believer is called to a life of obedience and dependence on God (Matthew 6:25-34, Philippians 4:6-7)
5) New Covenant believers are made a royal priesthood, and are called to witness to the nations God's goodness (Matthew 28:19-20, Mark 16:15, 1 Peter 2:9)

In conclusion, let me say one final word on salvation. **There is only one kind of person that God will save, the sinner kind!**

If you are not a sinner, than God can do nothing for you. You are eternally lost if you cannot recognize that you are in need of a Savior. The apostle Paul testified:

*"This is a faithful saying, and worthy of all acceptation, that **Christ Jesus came into the world to save sinners**; of whom I am chief."*
1 Timothy 1:15, KJV

Please do not let this day end before you confess that you are a sinner in need of a Savior, and give your heart to Jesus, who loves you and gave Himself for you.

Sin – The English word that translates the Hebrew word *"chata* - חטא*"* and the Greek word *"hamartia* – αμαρτια*"*. Both words mean to "miss the mark", "go wrong", and to "incur guilt". Sin is one of the few words that the Bible actually defines for itself. There are two definitions given.

1) Sin is the breaking of God's holy commandments

*"Whosoever committeth sin transgresseth also the law: for **sin is the transgression of the law**."*
1 John 3:4, KJV

Failing to live up to God's holy purposes for humanity is sin. Not doing what God says is right and/or doing what God says is wrong. Specifically, violation of the universal principles outlined in the 10 Divine Principles/Commandments, or the "Ten Words" in Hebrew (Exodus 20, Deut 5):
1) Put complete faith in Yahweh the God who delivers, put no gods before Yahweh, do not make idols/images of other "gods"
2) Do not bow down to idols or images of other "gods"
3) Do not take God's name (Yahweh) in vain – do not say you belong to God and then walk in disregard of His word, and do not use His name profanely and with disrespect
4) Keep the Sabbath (seventh) day holy, a day of rest
5) Honor your father and mother
6) Do not commit murder

7) Do not commit adultery
8) Do not steal
9) Do not give false testimony
10) Do not covet (desire lustfully) anything that belongs to someone else

Any honest person who just read that list knows they have broken at least one of these commandments, if not many of them. Jesus' brother James said:

"For whosoever shall keep the whole law, and yet offend in one point, he is guilty of all." James 2:10, KJV

Jesus said that the entire law and teaching of the prophets can be summarized by two great commandments found in Deuteronomy 6:5 and Leviticus 19:18:

*"Jesus said unto him, Thou shalt **love the Lord (Yahweh) thy God with all thy heart**, and with all thy soul, and with all thy mind. This is the first and great commandment. And the second is like unto it, Thou shalt **love thy neighbour as thyself**. On these two commandments hang all the law and the prophets."*

Matthew 22:37-40, KJV

2) Sin is the failure to put complete trust in the atonement offered in Christ

*"... for **whatsoever is not of faith is sin.**"*
Romans 14:23, KJV

In God's grace, He provided a means for humanity to receive atonement for their sins. **True faith trusts enough in God; in what he has said and promised, that you take action in obedience. When God says we have sinned, and He has, we take action to receive His forgiveness and atonement in Christ through repentance, then begin walking in a new life of obedience in the Holy Spirit.** In the Old Testament God provided that the repentant sinner could bring a sin offering (this offer extended beyond Israel to the nations as well, 1 Kings 8:41-43), and once a year the High Priest would offer an offering for the entire nation of Israel. These offerings were temporary, and foreshadowed the ultimate atonement for sin provided by Jesus the Messiah/Christ. Israel was promised a New Covenant.

"Behold, the days come, saith the LORD, that I will make a new covenant with the house of Israel, and with the house of Judah: Not according to the covenant that I made with their fathers in the day that I took them by the hand to bring them out of the land of Egypt; which my covenant they brake, although I was an husband unto them, saith the LORD: But this shall be the covenant that I will make with the house of Israel; After those days, saith the LORD, I will put my law in their inward parts, and write it in their hearts; and will be their God, and they shall be my people. And they shall teach no more every man his neighbour, and every man his brother, saying, Know the LORD: for they shall all know me, from the least of them unto the greatest of them, saith the LORD: for I will forgive their iniquity, and I will remember their sin no more." Jeremiah 31:31-34, KJV

And a consummate "lamb" that would bear sin was promised:

"Who hath believed our report? and to whom is the arm of the LORD revealed? For he

shall grow up before him as a tender plant, and as a root out of a dry ground: he hath no form nor comeliness; and when we shall see him, there is no beauty that we should desire him. He is despised and rejected of men; a man of sorrows, and acquainted with grief: and we hid as it were our faces from him; he was despised, and we esteemed him not. Surely he hath borne our griefs, and carried our sorrows: yet we did esteem him stricken, smitten of God, and afflicted. **But he was wounded for our transgressions, he was bruised for our iniquities: the chastisement of our peace was upon him; and with his stripes we are healed. All we like sheep have gone astray; we have turned every one to his own way; and the LORD hath laid on him the iniquity of us all.** *He was oppressed, and he was afflicted, yet he opened not his mouth: he is brought as a lamb to the slaughter, and as a sheep before her shearers is dumb, so he openeth not his mouth. He was taken from prison and from judgment: and who shall declare his generation? for he was cut off out of the land of the living: for the transgression of my people was he stricken. And he made his grave with the wicked, and with the rich in his* *death; because he had done no violence, neither was any deceit in his mouth." Isaiah 53:1-9, KJV*

Jesus Christ laid his life down as the final and eternal sacrifice for our sin, and brought in the New Covenant.

"For this is my blood of the new testament, which is shed for many for the remission of sins." Matthew 26:28, KJV

*"... we are sanctified through the offering of the body of Jesus Christ once for all. And every priest standeth daily ministering and offering oftentimes the same sacrifices, which can never take away sins: But this man, after he had offered one sacrifice for sins for ever, sat down on the right hand of God; From henceforth expecting till his enemies be made his footstool. **For by one offering he hath perfected for ever them that are sanctified**." Hebrews 10:10-14, KJV*

The real sin that condemns a person for all eternity is not the violation of any one of the 7 laws given to Noah (Jewish tradition regarding stipulations on all people after the flood), the 10 Commandments of Sinai (foundational principles for living a good life before God), or the 613 sub-commandments given to Israel through Moses (traditional Jewish numbering of all the requirements placed on Israel through Moses). The sin that condemns a person for all eternity is the rejection, unbelief, and lack of living faith in the means by which God has provided deliverance and atonement from the aforementioned sins; The death and resurrection of the Messiah, Jesus.

"For God so loved the world, that he gave his only begotten Son, that whosoever believeth in him should not perish, but have everlasting life. For God sent not his Son into the world to condemn the world; but that the world through him might be saved. He that believeth on him is not condemned: but he that believeth not is condemned already, because he hath not believed in the name of the only begotten Son of God." John 3:16-18, KJV

Satan – Fallen angelic being of the "cherub" class (Ezekiel 28:14) who is leader of an ongoing sedition against Yahweh and the

Adamic/human race created in Yahweh's image. Also know as "the serpent", "devil", Lucifer, shining one, and the "great dragon". He has angels, demons and humans (some wittingly, and some unwittingly) that are subservient to him, constituting the "kingdom of darkness", or the "kingdom of Satan". The term "*satan*" literally means "adversary", and was adapted as a title/name of the chief "adversary" of God and his people.

Jesus came to set people free from Satan's dominion by faith in the gospel of Christ's death, burial, and resurrection. Jesus exposed Satan for what he is.

Speaking to "religious" people who challenged Christ's authority, Jesus said:

"Ye are of your father the devil, and the lusts of your father ye will do. He was a murderer from the beginning, and abode not in the truth, because there is no truth in him. ***When he speaketh a lie, he speaketh of his own: for he is a liar, and the father of it.***"
John 8:44, KJV

Those that reject atonement and treat God's people with contempt, follow their leader into the lake of fire, which was not meant for people, but rather for Satan and his angels:

*"Then shall he say also unto them on the left hand, Depart from me, ye cursed, into **everlasting fire, prepared for the devil and his angels**:"*
Matthew 25:41, KJV

Satan can play the good guy in order to deceive:

"And no marvel; for Satan himself is transformed into an angel of light."
2 Corinthians 11:14, KJV

Jesus defeated Satan:

"He that committeth sin is of the devil; for the devil sinneth from the beginning. For this purpose the Son of God was manifested, that he might destroy the works of the devil."
1 John 3:8, KJV

A ruler comes at the end of the age that is directly allied with and indwelt by Satan:

"Even him, whose coming is after the working of Satan with all power and signs and lying wonders,"
2 Thessalonians 2:9, KJV

Satan and his angels are cast out of heaven to the earth:

"And the great dragon was cast out, that old serpent, called the Devil, and Satan, which deceiveth the whole world: he was cast out into the earth, and his angels were cast out with him."
Revelation 12:9, KJV

After the return of Jesus Christ to the earth, Satan is locked up for a thousand years of peace while Jesus rules and reigns:

"And he laid hold on the dragon, that old serpent, which is the Devil, and Satan, and bound him a thousand years,"
Revelation 20:2, KJV

Finally, Satan is cast into the lake of fire for all eternity:

"And the devil that deceived them was cast into the lake of fire and brimstone, where the beast and the false prophet are, and shall be tormented day and night for ever and ever." Revelation 20:10, KJV

This ends the glossary. I hope this was enough to back up the material in the body of this work, and clearly define key terms. Come to God the Father through faith in the sacrifice of His Son Jesus, through the conviction and truth of the Holy Spirit. Jesus is LORD, and our enemy is defeated. Hallelujah, praise His name forever!

Endnotes

[1] This truth was first brought to my attention by Bible teacher and Greek scholar Derek Prince in his teaching video:

Derek Prince, *Basics of Deliverance – Video Teaching.* Derek Prince Ministries, 1985.

This nuance of the Greek has since been validated by my own studies in Koine Greek.

[2] The reality of psychosomatic illness is easily researched, but I provide here a few links simply to validate the premise.

http://patient.info/health/psychosomatic-disorders (last accessed June 14, 2015)

https://en.wikipedia.org/wiki/Psychosomatic_medicine (last accessed June 14, 2015)

[3] English definitions derived in part from: The American Heritage Dictionary:

Second College Edition, Houghton Mifflin Company, Boston. 1982

[4] כי ביום אכלך ממנו מות תמות – "for in the day you eat from it, dying you will die"

[5] While interpretations vary regarding the Genesis 6 passage and the application of Jude 6 and 2 Peter 2:4-5, the oldest interpretations apply the Genesis passage to fallen angels cohabiting with human women which resulted in "demigods", "titans", or "giants". And so, 1st Century AD Jewish historian Josephus comments in "Antiquities of the Jews", Book I Chapter III:

1. NOW this posterity of Seth continued to esteem God as the Lord of the universe, and to have an entire regard to virtue, for seven generations; but in process of time they were perverted, and forsook the practices of their forefathers; and did neither pay those honors to God which were appointed them, nor had they any concern to do justice towards men. But for what degree of zeal they had formerly shown for virtue, they now showed by their actions a double degree of wickedness, whereby they made God to be their enemy. For many angels (11) of God accompanied with women, and begat sons that proved unjust, and despisers of all that was good, on account of the confidence they had in their own strength; for the tradition is, that these men did what resembled the acts of those whom the Grecians call giants. But Noah was very uneasy at what they did; and being displeased at their conduct, persuaded them to change their dispositions and their acts for the better: but seeing they did not yield to him, but were slaves to their wicked pleasures, he was afraid they would kill him, together with his wife and children, and those they had married; so he departed out of that land.

Worthy also, the translator W. Whiston adds this note (11), *"This notion, that the fallen angels were, in some sense, the fathers of the old giants, was the constant opinion of antiquity."*

Later alternative interpretations include interpreting the "Sons of God" of Genesis 6 as godly descendants of Seth taking wicked daughters of Cain, or more recently, rulers of early city states who claimed to be descended from deity exercising right of "first night", or just taking any woman they choose. Many in recent times have risen up to champion the classic understanding, perhaps among the most well know would be on the popular front, Stephen Quayle (www.stevequayle.com), on the biblical studies front, Dr. Chuck Missler (www.khouse.org), and on the scholarly front, Dr. Michael Heiser (www.drmsh.com and www.thedivinecounsel.com).

[6] The Book of Enoch, Translated by R.H. Charles. The Apocrypha and Pseudepigrapha of the Old Testament. H.R. Charles Oxford: The Clarendon Press, Chapter 15: verses 8-12.

Compiled in the 2nd century BCE from varied sources, The Book of Enoch was in common circulation during the period of the New Testament and for some time later, so, while not inspired scripture, it is useful to help determine what was understood by a reader/listener at that time. Enoch is even cited in the letter of Jude verse 14. Bible terms are to be understood by how the audience of the time was intended to understand them, and at the time they understood evil spirits, aka demons, to be the disembodied offspring of fallen angels and humans. Jesus never challenged this understanding. From the book of Enoch:

"8) And now, the giants, who are produced from the spirits and flesh, shall be called evil spirits upon 9) the earth, and on the earth shall be their dwelling. Evil spirits have proceeded from their bodies; because they are born from men and from the holy Watchers [governing angels, good or fallen], *is their beginning and primal origin; 10) they shall be evil spirits on earth, and evil spirits shall they be called. As for the spirits of heaven, in heaven*

shall be their dwelling, but as for the spirits of the earth which were born upon the earth, on the earth shall be their dwelling. And the spirits of the giants afflict, oppress, destroy, attack, do battle, and work destruction on the earth, and cause trouble: they take no food, but nevertheless 12) hunger and thirst, and cause offences. And these spirits shall rise up against the children of men and against the women, because they have proceeded from them."

http://www.ccel.org/c/charles/otpseudepig/enoch/ENOCH_1.HTM

[7] The book of Hebrews outlines how Christ fulfilled the foreshadowing of Old Testament sacrifices.

"The old system in the law of Moses was only a shadow of the things to come, not the reality of the good things Christ has done for us. The sacrifices under the old system were repeated again and again, year after year, but they were never able to provide perfect cleansing for those who came to worship. If they

could have provided perfect cleansing, the sacrifices would have stopped, for the worshipers would have been purified once for all time, and their feelings of guilt would have disappeared. But just the opposite happened.

Those yearly sacrifices reminded them of their sins year after year. For it is not possible for the blood of bulls and goats to take away sins. That is why Christ, when he came into the world, said, "You did not want animal sacrifices and grain offerings. But you have given me a body so that I may obey you. No, you were not pleased with animals burned on the altar or with other offerings for sin. Then I said, 'Look, I have come to do your will, O God--just as it is written about me in the Scriptures.'" Christ said, "You did not want animal sacrifices or grain offerings or animals burned on the altar or other offerings for sin, nor were you pleased with them" (though they are required by the law of Moses). Then he added, "Look, I have come to do your will." He cancels the first covenant in order to establish the second. And what God wants is for us to be made holy by the sacrifice of the body of Jesus Christ once for all time.

Under the old covenant, the priest stands before the altar day after day, offering sacrifices that can never take away sins. But our High Priest offered himself to God as one sacrifice for sins, good for all time. Then he sat down at the place of highest honor at God's right hand. There he waits until his enemies are humbled as a footstool under his feet. For by that one offering he perfected forever all those whom he is making holy."
Hebrews 10:1-14, NLT

[8] Credit is due Michael S. Heiser, PhD for his work in the area of the Divine council, and Yahweh among the lesser "gods". His work is a great help in coming to a better understanding of how the authors of scripture use the terms. Further research can be done at his web site: http://www.thedivinecouncil.com

Bibliography

Charles, R. H. (1912). *The Book of Enoch* : or 1 Enoch ; translated from the editor's Ethiopic text and edited with the introduction, notes and indexes of the first edition wholly recast, enlarged and rewritten, together with a reprint from the editor's text of the Greek fragments. Oxford, Clarendon Press.
Available Online: http://www.ccel.org/c/charles/otpseudepig/enoch/ENOCH_1.HTM

The American Heritage Dictionary: Second College Edition. Boston: Houghton Mifflin, 1982.

Josephus, Flavius and William Whiston. *The*

Life and Works of Flavius Josephus, the Learned and Authentic Jewish Historian and Celebrated Warrior, to Which Are Added Seven Dissertations Concerning Jesus Christ, John the Baptist, James the Just, God's Command to Abraham, Etc. Philadelphia: J. C. Winston Co., 1957.

Prince, Derek. *Basics of Deliverance – Video Teaching.* Derek Prince Ministries. Estimated initial release mid 1980s.

This video can be found on YouTube, and audio is available from Derek Prince Ministries website:
http://www.derekprince.org/Store/Products/1000034543/DPM_Store/MP3/Basics_of_Deliverance.aspx

As stated in the body, content was taken directly from notes written in my Bible when I first watched the video in 1988. I also had the privilege of witnessing Derek teach on deliverance in person in 1989 in Jerusalem, Israel.